AWAKEN

"This book is a MUST read for anyone who wants to be free from the anxiety that holds them back. Amy offers an intelligent approach to healing old wounds as well as inspiring stories that will show you how to live a much freer life."

—**Rachael Jayne Groover**,
Founder of The Awakened School and
Best-selling author of *Powerful and Feminine*

"Anyone who has lived with anxiety will instantly relate and be deeply moved by Amy's personal stories of her journey to overcome the negative forces in her life. The powerful tools she provides in her book facilitate our own awakening to our True Selves, allowing us to harness the creative power that resides within us. I highly recommend this book as a cherished resource for those who want to discover who they are, their unique soul's purpose, and how to share their inner light with others."

—**Andrea Cadelli**, author of *Life After This*

AWAKENING THROUGH ANXIETY

♥

A Journey to Finding
One's True Self

AMY BLAKESLEE

Copyright © 2021 Amy Blakeslee

All rights reserved. No part of this book may be reproduced by any mechanical, photographic, or electronic process, or in the form of phonographic recording: nor may it be stored in a retrieval system, transmitted, or otherwise be copied for public or private use, without prior written permission of the author.

For information about permission to reproduce
selections from this book, write to:
Calm Ocean Publishing
Redondo Beach, CA

Library of Congress Control Number: 9781641846790

ISBN 978-1-64184-679-0 paperback
ISBN 978-1-64184-680-6 ebook

Printed in the United States of America.

This book details the author's personal experiences with and opinions about recovering from anxiety and surviving childhood trauma. It is intended to provide helpful and informative material on the subjects it addresses. The author is not a healthcare provider. Please consult with your own physician or primary therapist regarding the suggestions and recommendations made in this book. The author and publisher specifically disclaim all responsibility for any liability, loss, or risk, personal or otherwise, that is incurred as a consequence, directly or indirectly, of the use and application of any of the contents of this book.

This book deals with intense and adverse childhood experiences, including domestic violence, mental abuse, substance abuse, and sexual abuse. While the author has taken great lengths to ensure the subject matter is dealt with in a compassionate and respectful manner, it may be troubling for some readers. Discretion is advised. The events of the author's life are portrayed to the best of the author's memory. The thoughts and feelings presented are the author's only. In order to maintain anonymity, names of individuals have been changed.

For Marilyn

To live in hearts we leave behind is not to die.
—Thomas Campbell

CONTENTS

INTRODUCTION	ix
1. CONNECTING TO OUR TRUE SELF	1
2. ANXIETY'S GRIP	6
3. WHEN YOU SUFFER, YOU SEEK	12
4. ENERGY IS EVERYTHING	16
5. OUR HEART IS THE CONNECTION TO OUR TRUE SELF	22
6. TRUE-SELF EXERCISES	24
METHOD: CONNECT TO YOUR HEART SPACE	25
METHOD: FEEL YOUR LIGHT WITHIN	27
METHOD: BEING PRESENT	32
7. CONNECTED CHILD	34
8. CHILDHOOD ADVERSITY	39
9. I AM A POWERFUL CREATOR	46
10. LIFE WITH DAD	49
11. BOUNDARIES	55
12. YOUR MIND IS AN AMAZING STORYTELLER	62

13. TRUE-SELF EXERCISE	69
METHOD: RELEASE TECHNIQUE	70
HEALING SYMPTOMS	72
REMEDIES	73
14. SHINE YOUR LIGHT	75
15. LIFE WITH MOM	80
16. MY DAD'S SUICIDE	87
17. A WHOLE NEW WORLD	94
18. FINAL DAYS	103
19. ON BEING A PARENT	110
20. LIGHT OF DIVINITY WITHIN	113
21. TRUE-SELF EXERCISES	115
METHOD: AFFIRMATIONS	115
METHOD: VISUALIZATION	119
METHOD: INTENTIONS	120
METHOD: RECEIVING	122
22. MY SHIFT TO INNER PEACE AND CALM	123
23. LONELINESS	125
24. MY (NOT SO GOOD) APPROACH TO FRIENDSHIP	134
25. MY RELATIONSHIP WITH MY SISTER	138
26. TRUE-SELF EXERCISE	142
METHOD: MEDITATION	142
27. KINDNESS OF STRANGERS	144
28. FROM HIGH SCHOOL DROPOUT TO COLLEGE GRADUATE	150

29.	TRUE-SELF EXERCISE	160
	METHOD: GRATITUDE	160
30.	HEALTH AND HEALING MYSELF	163
31.	RELATIONSHIPS	169
32.	TRUE-SELF EXERCISE	173
	METHOD: RELEASE TECHNIQUE FOR RELATIONSHIPS	173
33.	COURAGE & RESILIENCY	176
34.	FORGIVENESS	180
35.	LETTING GO	184
36.	TRUE-SELF EXERCISE	187
	PUTTING IT ALL TOGETHER	187
37.	OVERCOMING FEAR OF PUBLIC SPEAKING WITH TRUE-SELF EXERCISES	189
38.	YOUR LIFE WILL BECOME EXTRAORDINARY	193
ACKNOWLEDGEMENTS		197
RESOURCES		199
	LIFE ENERGY COACHING	199
	TRUE-SELF EXERCISE RECORDINGS	199
ABOUT THE AUTHOR		201

INTRODUCTION

At thirty-nine, I felt like I was on the brink of a complete nervous breakdown. On the outside looking in, I was living a charmed life. My then-husband was a good guy and a great dad. On the surface, we were a normal married couple. Our two young daughters were the center of my life. I was a technology leader for a major corporation, making a good income. We owned our own home, had money in the bank, food on the table, and all our material needs were met.

Except I was living a lie. The lie of not being true to myself. Deep within, I knew I wanted my life to be something different and I wanted to be somewhere else. I felt it all the time but didn't act on it. Instead, I went through the motions of going to work, taking my daughters on playdates, doing our weekly grocery shopping, and entertaining friends with dinner parties and cookouts. All normal things I approached in a normal way, but inside I was barely holding it together.

Ever since I could remember, I suffered from a deep, intense anxiety. It was almost debilitating at times, manifesting in unhealthy and uncomfortable ways. It was becoming harder and harder to keep under control. In fact, the more I tried to control it, the more intense it became. I didn't fully understand why I was experiencing it and why it was constantly with me.

This is my story of how I overcame this anxiety and became a powerful creator of my life. It's my journey from the hardships I experienced in my childhood to my transformation into the calm and peaceful person I am today. The suffering I lived with was so intense that it forced me to discover the truth of who I really am, who we all are. I learned how to heal the pain I was feeling within myself and how to create a life that is authentic for me.

By sharing my experience, I hope to help those who have experienced suffering from traumas to realize how powerful they really are. To move from feeling constant turmoil within our bodies to developing and maintaining inner peace. In this book, I've included techniques I practice regularly to remain in a peaceful state and to construct my life using the power we all have within ourselves.

I am so blessed to share my life story with you, from the ordeals of my childhood to the journey back to my True Self. I hope it inspires you to discover your True Self. We all have the ability to overcome negative life stories. We can shift from being a victim of circumstances to wielding the God-given gifts we all have to heal ourselves and to create a new, powerful, and positive life.

1

CONNECTING TO OUR TRUE SELF

♥

I've discovered that much of the pain we face in our lives comes because we are disconnected from who we really are, our True Self. The easiest way to connect back to your True Self is through your heart. The heart is our connection between the physical world and the spiritual world. Our hearts are the essence of who we are at the core of our being. Through our hearts, we connect to our inner wisdom, our higher self, and to the voice of God. Through our hearts, we connect to the power of love.

Decades of suffering caused me to search deeply and rediscover this part of myself. Over more than a decade, I worked with many teachers and coaches as I uncovered this truth. I spent thousands of hours studying every book I could get my hands on, and then putting into practice the teachings of many spiritual leaders and scientific experts. I regained the connection to my True Self that I once had as a small child, before the traumatic experiences of my life made me blind to my inner power.

CONNECTING TO OUR TRUE SELF

When we heal our heart, we open ourselves to receive incredible wisdom from the mighty power of All That Is. No matter what you call it – God, The Universe, Source, Infinite Power – it is all the same force. While I am not a religious person, I call this power God. I sometimes refer to it as The Universe or Source but having felt this infinite energy within myself, God is the only word that does it true justice. To me, any other name dilutes the real significance of this power.

Using the word God can spark many different reactions, especially from religious followers. I was not raised in a religious household and the only time you heard the mention of God in my house it was almost certainly followed by the words "damn it." My dad was a self-proclaimed atheist and my mom belonged to the Protestant church, but she did not practice religion. She would send me and my sister to Sunday School to get us out of her hair for an hour or two, but otherwise religion was not present at home. When I was thirteen, mostly because all my friends were doing it, I committed to joining our church and attended weekly confirmation classes. The format and teachings did not resonate with me, however, and the service where I was baptized and confirmed was the last one I attended.

Even at a young age, I sensed there were many limiting beliefs associated with the word "god". I felt it at our church and through my religious friends' actions and words. The stories I learned in Sunday school just never rang true for me and even seemed downright silly. God was portrayed as a bearded guy sitting in the sky, controlling our fate, and judging each of us by keeping track of when we were being good and when we were being bad. Favoring some but not others. To my six-year-old self, it felt as if there was no difference between God and Santa Claus.

Please know that I am not here to compete with or criticize any religion. What I am sharing with you is quite complementary to all religions whose basis comes from the highest frequency of love. For example, the Bible is full of parables that teach you how to play the game of life using some of the same methods I am sharing in this book. Jesus himself was a mystical, masterful energy worker, teaching through his healing of others by using the powerful vibration of love.

Regardless of how you feel about religion, I ask that you keep an open mind as you are introduced to the content of this book. Do the exercises, see how practical they are, and how much easier, joyful, loving, peaceful, and abundant your life can become. Let your experience lead you to your conclusion of this material.

I believe that God is not separate from us. God is omnipresent, omniscient, and omnipotent – all-being, all-knowing, and all-powerful. God is all. God is you. God is me. God is every person, every animal, every plant, the oceans, the moon, the sun, the stars, the planets, and the universe. God is the infinite everything there is, ever was, and ever will be.

My favorite analogy compares God to the ocean and each one of us are the individual drops of water that make up that ocean. Therefore, we too share the same traits of all-being, all-knowing, and all-powerful. We are all individual, yet we are one. God is experiencing itself through each of us. The trials, the tribulations, the happiness, and the joy. I believe the true purpose of all our lives is to awaken back to the God-state that is within each of us, our True Self, and that we are ultimately meant to live wonderful lives that are filled with love, joy, and bliss.

CONNECTING TO OUR TRUE SELF

Negative feelings we experience, such as shame, fear, anger, guilt, and hate, show us where we are out of alignment with the divinity we are. These feelings play an important role in our discovery back to our True Self. Without them we would not experientially know, respect, and fully honor the good within each of us.

You are a divine being created in the likeness and image of God. While you may have trouble believing these words, you can feel this is true on a level deep within you. You can feel this truth in your being. Connecting back to your heart will lead you to this truth. Here you will find the good you are seeking. You will discover freedom from suffering and start experiencing the divine gifts of Love, Inner Peace, Joy, and Purpose. When you connect to your heart, you will clearly hear the inner wisdom from within and start creating your life from this divine connection.

Throughout this book, I will refer to our life energy. Everything is energy. Ki, Chi, and Prana are all names for this energy. We can use tools to change our life energy to heal ourselves and to create the world we wish to experience. The key is to transform all that is negative within us back to love. We will come to a place of inner peace, where we can connect with our heart and create our lives from this sacred space.

If you are reading this book, you may have either started on your awakening path to know your True Self, or this book is your call to begin the discovery. You may initially react to some or all of this content with skepticism, disbelief, or anger. You may even find it comical, which is not an unusual reaction. I initially had my own doubts about much of this, too. At first, it's hard to conceive that the simple exercises I am sharing with you could drastically change your life and that you do not always need a doctor, a therapist, or drugs to heal yourself.

I ask that you stay open-minded and try the exercises before dismissing them outright. You may find that when you apply the techniques in this book, you will easily experience positive and lasting change within yourself. You will effortlessly create your own miracles as you create an extraordinary life.

We live on a beautiful planet with many wonders happening every day. If we open our awareness to them, we will see them all the time. Our world would be even more amazing if we all lived from our True Selves. My hope is that you will experience this connection while doing the True-Self exercises in this book. From here, you can live from the divine power of love. Your life will change in magical ways. And for that you can trust in God.

2

ANXIETY'S GRIP

♥

As far back as I can remember, I lived with anxiety and a deep sense of fear that was with me all the time. My early life experiences of abuse and trauma caused me to live in a constant state of fight or flight mode. I was always on the lookout for danger, perceived or real, ready to move quickly out of harm's way. Anxiety was a constant part of who I was. Like breathing or my heartbeat, it was a persistent buzz of inner turmoil that I felt within my whole being.

Growing up in an unsafe environment with little ability to change my circumstances turned me into an adult who had to control everything in life. I was vigilant about my emotional, mental, and physical safety. My life choices were always made from this context. Moving away from something because I was afraid always won out over moving toward what I really wanted. I was a relentless worrier, dwelling with fear on the smallest of topics. I played over and over in my mind all the things that could go wrong in the future, and I damned myself for everything I should have done differently in the past.

I was so consumed with wanting to stay safe that I didn't really know who I was or what I really wanted. I wasn't honest with myself about the depth of my anxiety, instead putting on a façade of strength. I certainly did not share my anguish with other people because I was afraid that my tough exterior would crack wide open and I would have to face what was underneath.

I felt like I was defective and alone in my pain. Having an anxiety disorder is not something you casually talk about with others, especially since bringing attention to oneself can exacerbate the condition. Only my ex-husband and a couple of close friends knew what I was dealing with.

Today I know that I was not unique, not by any means. According to the Anxiety and Depression Association of America, 40 million American adults, or approximately 20% of the U.S. adult population, suffer from an anxiety disorder. One in five adults you come across are dealing with a form of this common mental illness and most are doing everything they can to keep it hidden from others. These are the silent sufferers, those like me who don't want to face it and are too afraid to seek help. People who seem normal on the outside but are battling this affliction within.

While I was never diagnosed, I believe I was afflicted with both post-traumatic stress syndrome (PTSD) and social anxiety. My symptoms manifested often and in many uncomfortable ways. In my near constant state of fight-or-flight response, I would often catch myself holding my breath while tensing my body from head to toe, even when I was by myself. I had difficulty sleeping as I tossed and turned while furiously grinding my teeth all night. I woke up most mornings feeling exhausted, my jaw sore from the constant pressure. I developed many dental problems which only added to the constant cycle of worry.

The most visible and embarrassing symptom of my anxiety was severe underarm sweating, which is a form of hyperhidrosis. Hyperhidrosis is a physical condition of increased sweating that affects about 5% of the population and has a deep, negative impact on the emotional and social quality of one's life. It showed up the most when I was in social situations or in the presence of authority figures. There are topical medications that can be used to reduce the sweating, but they caused my sensitive skin to burn and itch, so I rarely used them. I also tried Botox injections, but they didn't work well enough to justify the high cost. More often than not, I controlled the visibility of the sweat stains through my wardrobe, choosing dark clothes that camouflaged the sweating as best as possible.

More than once while on a job interview, my anxiety levels were so high that I sweated all the way through my shirt and my suit jacket. The first time it happened I was wearing a gray suit and the dark, wet stains on the outside of the jacket were visible when I moved my arms. I was mortified since I most wanted to project calm, cool and confidence to impress my interviewer. Of course, my horror only compounded the feelings of anxiety and caused me to sweat more, creating a vicious circle I could not escape.

When I was highly anxious, my hands would shake uncontrollably. This was the ultimate betrayal by my physical body and I always felt ashamed of myself when it occurred. At its worst, the shaking became so intense I couldn't hold on to anything without a tight grip. Although these episodes were rare, I was reluctant to do any activity with my hands in front of other people. I avoided social situations that required participation in activities. Scared to be seen shaking and sweating, I lived in constant fear of being judged and ostracized.

For almost two decades, I lived on-and-off with the irrational fear of not being able to sign my name in front of anyone without my hands shaking uncontrollably. The first time I experienced this was at the DMV right after I was married, when I applied for a new driver's license with my new last name. The clerk asked me to sign the application form in front of her. It was the first time I was legally signing my married name, and suddenly I felt nervous.

After that incident, my mind began associating signing my name as an anxiety-inducing event. Depending on my inner state and who was present, my hands would shake when I signed my name. The level of fear I was feeling would dictate the readability of my signature. When I was highly stressed, the letters looked cramped and jagged while I tried to control the pen on the paper. I did everything I could to avoid writing my signature in the presence of others. The mere thought of doing it could even cause me to hyperventilate.

This irrational fear caused me to miss out on opportunities such as international travel, because I was too afraid to sign my name in front of the immigration clerk to renew my passport. I put off starting a business for years because I was afraid to sign my name on the official documents in front of the notary public. Signing a credit card slip in front of a store clerk proved traumatic, as I tried to control the irrational fear within me. I didn't know what to do. I could mentally work through the phobia in my conscious mind, but I did not know how to talk to my body.

My whole adult life became centered on this anxiety that arose from the adverse childhood experiences I'll share later in this book. As a child and young adult, the anxiety seemed easier to cope with since I didn't have to put myself on the line for others. There just wasn't as much at stake for me personally or professionally. When my responsibilities increased, my anxiety grew, taking on a life of its own.

I was vigilant in trying to control my anxiety, trying my hardest to make it unnoticeable to anyone else. Therefore, I avoided situations that intensified it, especially in my technology career. While I had the experience and the brains, I initially shied away from the top leadership positions that required public speaking and standing up for your position on key topics. Instead, I kept myself stuck in middle-management longer than I should have, just so I wouldn't have to face the painful feelings.

I made excuses about why I was holding myself back. "I want to stay technical and hands-on," was my response when I was offered positions of leadership early in my career. It was only partly true. I found the engineering work I was doing to be creative and fulfilling, but there was a part of me that longed to step boldly into the leadership roles I secretly desired. Some of my other favorite lines included: "I don't want to deal with office politics," "I don't want to put in the extra hours," and "I don't like the boss I would report to." At the height of my anxiety, most choices I made came from the place of keeping myself from feeling fear, rather than boldly stepping toward my dreams and desires.

When I was thirty-four, I finally mustered up the courage to go to a therapist named Al. Right off the bat, he wanted to prescribe anti-anxiety medication to combat my symptoms, but I refused. I am not a fan of drugs in general; I rarely take over-the-counter medications. Growing up, I saw my brother struggle with drug addiction for many years. Watching this habit take over his life and control his personality made me afraid that I, too, could grow dependent on these substances. I also believe I knew deep down there was a different way, a better way, to heal myself. I just didn't know what that was yet.

Al gave me some CDs with guided meditations for relaxation. The meditations provided some relief, but I had no discipline at the time to establish a regular practice. I would occasionally do a meditation at night before bed, but most of the time I would forget I had the recordings. At the time, I did not understand the benefit of meditation for self-healing like I do now.

Talking to Al helped somewhat but I wasn't entirely forthcoming about everything that had caused the angst within me. Even though I still felt a great deal of anxiety, after about eight sessions we both decided I no longer needed to see him. I was still strongly controlling myself and my feelings, so I never really gave Al a chance. He probably knew I could not make progress until I was ready to open up. And there was no way I was going to let go any time soon.

3

WHEN YOU SUFFER, YOU SEEK

I was thirty-nine and it was a normal Saturday like any other. I was in the kitchen and I picked up a magazine my then-husband had left lying on the counter. It was opened to the book-review section and I was immediately drawn to an assessment of *The Secret* by Rhonda Byrne. *The Secret* describes how we all have the ability to intentionally and effortlessly create a joyful life using the Law of Attraction. According to *The Secret*, under the Law of Attraction everything you experience in your life comes through the magnetic power of your thoughts. Through the Law of Attraction, like attracts like. What you think and feel about, you bring into your life.

The magazine review was lukewarm at best, the reviewer obviously skeptical about the concepts it presented. Even so, as I read the review, I felt an excitement and a stirring within my being that I could not ignore. I felt this book held answers that could ease my pain.

I brought the article immediately to my husband. "I have to get this book now," I told him with a sense of urgency. I bought the book that very day and read it cover to cover in less than twenty-four hours. My life was forever changed. This was the start of my awakening.

The Secret opened up new and foreign ideas of reality for me. At first the concepts were difficult for my mind to grasp:

Thoughts become things.
I create my own reality.
I can change my life just by changing how I think and feel about it.
"I AM," are the two most powerful words that shape your life experience.

Growing up with no control over the adverse circumstances created by the adults in my life, the idea that I could actually influence my reality was mind-blowing. But regardless of what my mind was saying, I had a feeling in my body that I was on to something big.

I decided right then and there I would start first thing Monday morning by changing how I approached work. My job was a major source of anxiety for me and I always dreaded the start of the workweek. Like many other people, I would begin to feel uneasy and sick to my stomach on Sunday evenings. Sometimes it would sneak in on Saturdays, completely robbing me of a weekend of relaxation and fun with my kids.

When I awoke Monday morning, I told myself it was going to be a great day. I kept repeating "it's a great day" over and over again as I got ready for work, drove to my office building, and walked into the lobby. I got in the elevator and a man I sometimes talked to also jumped on board. He looked at me and said, "Ugh, another day in this hell," grimacing to add extra emphasis to his words.

WHEN YOU SUFFER, YOU SEEK

He looked at me expectantly, waiting for my agreement to the horrors that awaited us. Instead, I turned to him and smiled while exclaiming, "I don't know about you, but I think today is going to be a great day!" I left him standing there with his mouth open while I exited the elevator. Throughout the day, I kept that mantra going in my head and, to my delight, I ended up having a really good day at work.

As I practiced the exercises shared in *The Secret*, I experienced immediate, positive results in my life. I was able to influence how I felt by changing how I perceived my reality. For the first time in my life, I started to feel the intense grip of my anxiety loosening. It felt so good to have a respite from this constant suffering. This relief hinted at the power we have to create a different reality.

I was so excited by what I experienced that I started to follow this approach on an on-going basis. It wasn't easy to develop these skills as old habits die hard. It still can be a challenge for me today. We live in a world where the majority of people do not gravitate toward positivity, love, and personal creation. Instead, most feel victim to something or someone else, feeling they have little choice but to live with the hand they were dealt. It's so easy to get caught up in the stories of negativity, fear, and lack. Breaking free requires commitment, discipline, and practice.

When you suffer, you seek. And my suffering ran deep. The initial lessons from *The Secret* were just enough for me to glimpse the possibility of my True Self. I spent the next ten years searching everywhere, hungry for all the information I could get my hands on, in my quest to really know myself and fully ease my pain.

I consumed hundreds of books and completed tens of online programs from some of the most well-known authors, doctors, scientists, and spiritual teachers in the world. I sought out one-on-one coaching from some of the best spiritual and life energy coaches. I learned how to connect the spiritual concepts to our physical world through books on quantum physics, life energy, and biology. I was relentlessly driven to find the answers and apply them to my life.

I discovered the effect that our beliefs, both good and bad, have on creating our reality. What we believe is continuously reflected back to us, thanks to the Law of Attraction. When our beliefs are positive, we encounter positive events. When our beliefs are negative or limiting, our experiences are not so good. Because we are all powerful creators of our own reality, our beliefs will show up in our life over and over again. It may seem life is confirming to you what you believe is true when, in fact, it is only reflecting your own beliefs back at you. When you change your beliefs, what you experience will change.

When situations, healings, or events show up that are contrary to our limited beliefs, we call them miracles. What if I told you everything is a miracle? Everything that shows up in this life, good or bad, shows up because it was created based on the powerful beliefs we hold. We only label something a miracle when the result is positive and larger than our conscious beliefs.

4

ENERGY IS EVERYTHING

———— ♥ ————

Everything is energy, it is everywhere, and everything is connected. It's everything in the world we live in. It's you, it's me, and it's even our thoughts and feelings. This is a scientific fact confirmed by quantum physics, and it is also a spiritual truth. I will not go deep into the specifics of energy in this book. For spiritual seekers, there are many books about energy and related topics such as the Law of Attraction. For the science buffs, books on the subject of quantum physics and epigenetics delve deep into this topic. Bruce Lipton's *Biology of Beliefs* and books by Gregg Braden bridge spirituality and science. New materials are frequently published as more is discovered on these groundbreaking topics.

For everyone else, I think it's most important to understand the principle that everything is energy, and we have the ability to transform this energy to change our lives. The use of life energy healing techniques and heart-based exercises allows us to heal many times faster than using traditional medical approaches. Through these modalities, we can heal ourselves within seconds, hours, or days instead of months, years, or lifetimes. Yes, this is a very bold statement, but my story is a walking testimonial to the power of these modes of healing.

God is another term for this energy. Most of us lack awareness of this side of ourselves, which is our true nature. We see God as separate from us, on the outside of who we really are. We know ourselves solely as our body and our mind. We pay attention to our spiritual side only during limited, scheduled times like weekly church services or a daily meditation. But we are eternal in spirit. Our minds and bodies are for our temporary use on this planet, to navigate the physicality of this world. When we die, we shed our mind and body, but we persist as the eternal divine energy that we are.

When we are unaware of the spiritual side of our being, we go through life feeling an emptiness within. This feeling causes us to look outside of ourselves for our needs. There are many ways we try to fill this gap. We may look to others to give us love and affirm our worthiness. Some people overspend on material items, such as cars and clothes. Others may turn to food, alcohol, or drugs. Yet others use constant physical activity to distract them or fill up by binge-watching programs on Netflix.

One day, we will all wake up and recognize that inherently we are the spirit of God. When we begin to know ourselves as this divine energy, we open up to a whole new way of being and creating our lives. This is what life is all about.

Prior to awakening, most of us live in a negative state, coming from a sense of lack because we do not recognize our true, powerful, energetic nature. Much of the world today is operating on a negative frequency, where the dominant emotions come from fear, anger, hate, and shame. When we know ourselves as our True Selves, we can transform our energy to heal our problems and create a truly abundant, joyful life. We can live on the high frequencies of love, joy, and bliss.

On earth, in its current energetic composition, we come into contact with many negatively charged energies. They lure us in and hold us captive. It's much harder to be released from them. Think about how much easier it is to move from feeling happy to sad than from sad to happy. Negative emotions suck us in, and our Ego Mind loves to wallow in them. Only the powerful energy of love can transform this negativity into positive frequencies.

We all can shift our energy to the higher powers of love and joy. We really don't have a choice. The planet's vibration is changing, forcing us to move from the dense energies of the 3rd Dimension of consciousness to the higher frequencies of the 5th Dimension. This change will require all of us to awaken to our True Selves, forcing us to leave our negative personas behind.

Does this mean that as we ascend from one dimension to the next, we will physically move into a different world? Not exactly. Each dimension is a reflection of the consciousness one holds. We are all living within the same reality, but the way it is perceived and what you experience is entirely different based on the dimension you are aligned to.

The 3rd Dimension is related to the physical world, to what you can see, hear, touch, taste, and smell. Everything is separate and there is a limited supply to support the entire population. You often view yourself as a victim with a need to compete with others to survive. You judge everything and everyone as good or bad. In the 3rd Dimension there is much fear, and you are driven mainly by your Ego

Mind. It is easy to be manipulated by others when you are not rooted in the truth of who you really are.

In The 4th Dimension, you begin to awaken to the possibility there is more to life (and you) than meets the eye as your attention shifts toward the spiritual world. You begin to pursue knowledge and you start to understand the connectedness of life. However, you may feel anger toward the former way you lived. You may feel superior to those who are still living in the 3rd Dimension, judging them as being "asleep." You view your Ego Mind as the bad guy when you become aware of the role it has played in creating undesirable results in your life.

In the 5th Dimension, you know and experience the divinity that lies within you, your True Self. You live from a higher perspective, understanding love is the only real power. You live in a state of happiness and joy. You become aware that all is one, and there is no separateness. You accept others are on their own path. You no longer fight what shows up in your reality because you know what appears in your world is only a reflection of what lies within you. You work on healing yourself instead of trying to forcibly change the outer world. You create your reality from this powerful place.

Most of the people on the planet today are living in the 3rd Dimension, but a growing number are ascending to the 4th Dimension. A small percentage are already living fully from the 5th Dimension. The rise from the 3rd Dimension is evidenced in the disruption we are seeing in our society today, most prominently in the global coronavirus pandemic and in the world of politics. Survival fears are coming into awareness so we can collectively begin to heal and transform our world to the highest frequency of love.

ENERGY IS EVERYTHING

Energy has no physical boundaries. It has a vibrational force that reaches around the world. One person who is vibrating with love can immediately change the atmosphere of a room and the feelings of everyone in his or her presence. You will have the opportunity to experience this phenomenon yourself when you practice the exercises in this book. As you shift into True-Self awareness and really begin to embody this power, you will attract more loving and joyful events. Once you learn how to use your energy in positive ways, you will be surprised at how easy it is to create the life of your dreams.

Our life experiences are created by us, and we are always manifesting the best life we can based on our current level of consciousness. As you are introduced to these concepts, do not beat yourself up for having generated conditions in the past that have been less than loving, abundant, healthy, and joyful. Some circumstances are defined by the eternal you before you came into this existence, specifically for you to expand your consciousness through the reaction you have to experiences in this lifetime. Others manifest because you don't yet understand the power you have within yourself.

Growing in consciousness requires us to heal and let go of past traumas and hurt. We all store a great deal of negatively charged energy within our bodies, and its low vibration ends up creating adverse life experiences over and over. It shows up in our lives as poor health, unfulfilling relationships, lack of money, and other recurring dramas.

My anxiety was my wake-up call to heal. With decades of pent-up negative emotions stuck in my body, I was like a pressure cooker ready to explode. The energy desperately needed an outlet, choosing to relieve itself through my anxiety, my sweating, and my shaking. The symptoms were begging me to wake up and connect with my True Self.

Letting go of negative energy is the best thing you can do for yourself. The exercises in this book will teach you how to release and transform your life energy on your own. However, for the fastest transformation, it is most beneficial to do this work with a life energy coach, because they can hold space for you from their clear and high vibration. They've already done the work to align to their True Self and can easily guide you through the process.

We can each shift to a higher plane to bring more healing, love, and joy to ourselves and to this planet. We can bring peace to the world by developing our own inner peace and connection to our True Self. We can create a phenomenal life that truly reflects our power. This is such an exciting proposition!

By practicing the methods I share with you in this book, you will get to know the divine aspect of your True Self, raise your vibration, and develop your creative powers. If everyone were to do this, our planet would become a truly wondrous place to live.

5

OUR HEART IS THE CONNECTION TO OUR TRUE SELF

♥

My anxiety had a stronghold in my heart space, the area that is your whole center chest and includes your heart. My body never got a break from this feeling of constant turmoil. It was such an intense and constant part of my everyday existence that I thought it was naturally part of who I was. It distracted me from everything good in my life. It was the feeling that came before the other symptoms of anxiety and made it hard to focus on anything else. It truly was painful and I wanted it to end more than anything.

While I cursed my body for most of my life, I now know it was doing everything it was built to do. It was alerting me to where I was out of alignment with my True Self. It was showing me how disconnected I was to love.

As I started to focus on clearing the energy in my heart space, the love I felt for myself and others began to increase. I was exposed to the feelings of pure joy from within for the first time in my life! I could more clearly and more often hear this powerful voice of intuition, our connection to God and our True Self. I found it easier to attract all the good I wanted. I felt powerful and really alive for the first time in my life.

Connecting to our heart and cultivating inner peace is the doorway to becoming a conscious creator from within. Through this union, we can experience the limitless potential that lies within each of us. How powerful we are! And knowing this, how can we not let ourselves shine and trust in our authentic power?

6

TRUE-SELF EXERCISES

———— ♥ ————

As you practice the exercises in this book, I recommend you keep a journal, recording your before-and-after experiences. Transformation with these techniques can occur easily and sometimes their effect is very subtle. You will often not notice you have changed in a positive way or attracted something amazing unless you are reminded of your "before" state. Plus, it's really gratifying to go back and see on paper the progress you have made in getting to know your True Self and becoming a conscious creator of your life.

In the Resources section of this book, you will find a link to my recordings of the True-Self Exercises. Using recordings will allow you to focus fully and continually on the experience in a relaxed state, instead of reading each step from the book while practicing the method.

Most of all, have fun with these techniques and go easy on yourself! We are here to live a joyous and fulfilling life. When you focus on healing and transforming from a place where the energy is light and loving, your results will come much faster than approaching it from a place of resistance.

Method: Connect to Your Heart Space

It's one thing for me to tell you about your True Self, but to really know it you need to embody it. This means to feel who you are, really feel it, from the inside of your body. The simple practice of connecting to your heart space will give you a glimpse into your magnificence in just a matter of minutes.

You can do this exercise anywhere and at any time. I recommend repeating it often throughout your day, from the moment you wake up until you go to bed at night. There is no time limit required. You can spend 1, 5, or 50 minutes, whatever works for you. If you are like me, you will find this method brings so much joy to your being that you will repeat it often and for as long as possible each time.

The first time you do this exercise, it's important to put your full focus on the sensations within your body. Therefore, I recommend going to a place where you won't be disturbed. Get comfortable in the best way for you, it doesn't matter if you are standing, sitting, or lying down.

How to Connect to Your Heart Space:

1. Start out by taking a few breaths. Breathe in and out as you normally do, in the manner most comfortable for you.
2. Next, take a slow, deep breath through your nose. Feel the air as it moves down your throat, through

TRUE-SELF EXERCISES

      your lungs, and into your stomach. Hold this breath for a moment.
3. As you slowly breathe out, feel the air move from your stomach, into your lungs, through your throat and out your mouth.
4. Repeat breathing deeply in and out three more times. You should be feeling relaxed at the end of the fourth breath.
5. Continue to breathe normally while putting your attention on your heart space. This is the space is in the center of your chest that includes your heart. Note: It is important to breathe normally. Do not stop your breath at your heart space as doing so may cause you to hyperventilate.
6. Continue breathing and focusing on your heart space for as long as you wish. Revel in this powerful feeling that is connected to the essence of your True Self.

Current issues or past painful memories may come into your awareness while you are focusing on your heart space. Our hearts are where many of us hold the pain from past trauma and heartbreak. If this happens to you, know that this is okay. Keep breathing and focusing on your heart space. Later, I will be sharing the Release Technique, which is a method of letting go of the pain and suffering we feel in our bodies.

My heart space was the hardest for me to clear. Because I looked for love from others who didn't have the capacity to show me love, I spent much of my life feeling disconnected from it. As a child, neither my parents nor any other adult ever once said to me, "I love you," and they rarely hugged me. It's not surprising I carried so much pain in this space of my body. Doing this exercise helped to release that hurt and connect me back to my True Self.

Method: Feel Your Light Within

While practices like meditation are gaining in popularity today, most people still do not stop to take the time to really feel the entirety of who they are. Life is a constant grind of work with little time for relaxation and play. Our busyness keeps us in an unconscious state since we rarely have time to pause for self-reflection. With all our focus on the outer world, it's easy to see why we can't seem to get the time to be with our True Self. To become powerful creators of our life, it's important we stop doing and start being. Which means we need to get out of our mind and into our body.

The following exercise starts with first "Connect to Your Heart Space" before taking you deeper through your body. It will have you feeling your wholeness from within. For many of you, this will be the first time you have really paid attention to your entire physical being. In your new awareness, you may discover pain in your body that was hidden from your previous state of being. It will feel uncomfortable but know this is the start of healing pain from the past. With time and practice, you will come to love the relief this exercise gives you, and you will likely seek to practice it as often as possible.

I practice this exercise during meditation, when I am feeling stressed, when I first wake up, and before I go to bed at night. It keeps me anchored to my True Self, which is a truly wonderful way to live.

At first, it's best to do this privately, where you will not be disturbed. You should allow yourself a minimum

TRUE-SELF EXERCISES

of 15 minutes. Make yourself comfortable, either standing, lying down, or sitting up, but do not hunch over. It's important that you are in a position where you can feel your attention move freely through your body. While the attention of your "inhales" will shift during this exercise, the "exhales" should be done normally, feeling the air come up through your stomach, into your heart space, up your throat, and out your mouth.

How to Feel Your Light Within:

- Begin with the "Connect to Your Heart Space" exercise.
- Once you have connected to your heart space, picture a brilliant golden light coming down from about two feet above your head. This is a healing light. As you breathe in, visualize it entering your body through the crown of your head.
- As you continue breathing, move your attention down through your head, feeling the golden light permeate your forehead, your eyes, and in through your sinuses. Exhale.
- Breathe in again, feel the light coming into your cheeks, into your mouth, and stopping in your jaw. Exhale.
- Pause for a moment while you put your attention on the inside of your head all at once.
- Thoughts and feelings may be coming up for you. Notice them but don't try to change them, just observe what's going on. Let them be and let them go while you focus on your inner body.

- Breathe in again and feel the light move from your jaw down into your throat. You can spend another breath or two here, feeling the light swirl around in your throat.
- Inhale, moving the brilliant golden light into your shoulders.
- On your next breath, focus on the light moving into your left shoulder, feeling the energy go down your left arm and into your left hand. Exhale.
- Breathe in again, move the golden light back up your hand, through your arm, into your left shoulder, and pause at your neck. Exhale.
- On your next breath, focus on the light moving into your right shoulder, feeling the energy go down your right arm and into your right hand. Exhale.
- Breathe in again, move the golden light back up your hand, through your arm, into your right shoulder, and pause at your neck. Exhale.
- As you move your attention to your chest, breathe the golden light into this part of your body. Keep breathing while you focus on your lungs, your upper back, and shoulder blades.
- Next, move into your heart space. Breathe in and out, feeling the brilliant golden light filling up this part of your body.
- Thoughts and feelings may be coming up for you. Notice them but don't try to change them, just observe what's going on. Let them be and let them go while you focus on your inner body.
- Breathe as you move the golden light from your chest into your stomach. Breathe a few times

here as you feel the golden light swirling within your stomach.
- Exhale and feel the golden light move into your lower back.
- Now focus on your tailbone and pelvic area. Keep breathing while you feel the golden light penetrate this area. Spend a moment feeling the golden light swirl and permeate this entire part of your being. Exhale.
- Thoughts and feelings may be coming up for you. Notice them but don't try to change them, just observe what's going on. Let them be and let them go while you focus on your inner body.
- As you focus on your lower body, picture the golden light from above moving through each part of your body as you breathe in and out as follows:
    - Breathe in as the light moves within both glutes. Breathe out.
    - Breathe in, feel the light moving into your left hip. Breathe out.
    - Breathe in, feel the light moving through your left thigh. Breathe out.
    - Breathe in, feel the light moving into your left knee. Breathe out.
    - Breathe in, feel the light moving through your left calf. Breathe out.
    - Breathe in, feel the light moving into your left ankle. Breathe out.
    - Breathe in, feel the light moving into your left foot. Breathe out.
    - Pause for a moment while you feel the inside of your left leg all at once.

- - Thoughts and feelings may be coming up for you. Notice them but don't try to change them, just observe what's going on. Let them be and let them go while you focus on your inner body.
  - Put your attention back on your glutes.
  - Breathe in as the light moves within both glutes. Breathe out.
  - Breathe in, feel the light moving into your right hip. Breathe out.
  - Breathe in, feel the light moving through your right thigh. Breathe out.
  - Breathe in, feel the light moving into your right knee. Breathe out.
  - Breathe in, feel the light moving through right calf. Breathe out.
  - Breathe in, feel the light moving into your right ankle. Breathe out.
  - Breathe in, feel the light moving into your right foot. Breathe out.
  - Pause for a moment while you feel the inside of your right leg all at once.
  - Thoughts and feelings may be coming up for you. Notice them but don't try to change them, just observe what's going on. Let them be and let them go while you focus on your inner body.
- Keep breathing as you now feel your entire body all at once illuminated with this brilliant golden light.
- Stay here and relish this feeling for as long as you would like, breathing deeply, in and out.

Method: Being Present

Being present is the act of being in our body in the current moment. It takes us out of our mind, which is usually focused on the past or the future. How often are you in the moment? Most of us are off somewhere else, lost in our thoughts, worrying about what tomorrow might bring, or dwelling on a past situation that we can no longer change. Our attention is in our head space and we are not aware of the rest of our body. In this state, we are accessing only a fraction of our powerful self.

How to Practice Being Present:

You can easily become present once you are familiar with being in your body by doing the "Feel Your Light Within" exercise. You do not need to be alone when you do this exercise. In fact, the best way to practice it is during everyday activities. You can do it anywhere, for instance while attending a work meeting, standing in line at the store, eating dinner, talking to your spouse, working out, or going to bed at night. When you are focused in your body, you are able to experience what is really happening in the current moment.

You can practice being present by focusing on your whole body at once or by choosing a part of your body to tune into, similar to the "Connect to Your Heart Space" exercise. While you are being present, observe what comes up but do not attach to it with your mind. Feelings may move around your body and thoughts will beg for your attention. Just let them come and go.

If you practice being present as often as you can, you will soon see a positive shift in your perception of yourself and the world around you. You will become aware of how you have been existing on autopilot, letting random thoughts and feelings create your experience, whether you like it or not. You will be calmer with a knowing that the only place to really live is from the awareness of what is happening in the current moment. You will develop the ability to course-correct in the now and consciously choose your thoughts to deliberately create your life.

7

CONNECTED CHILD

♥

When I was a very small child, I felt the connection to my True Self. Before the outer voices of the physical world came in to change my view of myself and the world around me, I was happy, and I saw my life as abundant. I found great joy in playing outside on a warm rainy day, riding my Big Wheel around the block, and feeling the wind on my face while swinging at the park. I wanted everyone else to feel this way, too.

When my friends were hungry or hurt, I would sneak them into my house to offer up some bologna or a Band-Aid. My mom did not approve of my generosity and soon put a stop to it. She was deeply trapped in the illusions of the reality we were living. We were poor and there wasn't enough to feed our own family, much less some neighborhood kid who had their own parents to take care of them.

I didn't understand my mom's reaction to my generosity. I felt like my family was the richest in the world. I had toys, clothes, friends, and the abundant outdoors to play in freely. I loved our two dogs and I had many stuffed animals I cuddled up with every night.

I remember declaring our wealth to my sister Cheryl one day when I was about five years old. She looked at me with a mixture of disgust and incredulity. "No, we are not rich. We are dirt poor," she spat out.

Cheryl's forceful response shocked me deep into my core and shattered my world. I started to question everything I thought I knew. Where I had once felt so abundant, I began to see she was right about our family's situation. We were very poor. My alcoholic father would often spend much of his paycheck drinking at the tavern. It was not unusual to barely have enough food to feed our family.

Our toys and clothes usually came from yard sales. My dad made frequent trips to the city dump and sometimes scavenged through other people's garbage on trash day, looking for salvageable toys, furniture, and other household items. We would greet his finds with excitement at having something new, at least new for us. I guess it's true that some people's trash can be other people's treasures.

When we were young children, our dad's family gave us many toys at Christmas time. It was so exciting going to our aunt and uncle's house because we knew they would be generous with gifts our parents could not afford. Our excitement was short-lived, however. As soon as we got home, our parents would let us keep only a few of the toys. The rest were either returned to the store from which they were purchased or placed in the attic to be sold in our garage sale the following summer.

I look back at the pictures of my young self and, while the color is faded from time gone by, a brightness emanates from me. I was a skinny girl, small for my age, with long golden hair, squinty eyes, and a big smile. Very shy,

I attracted attention wherever I went. People wanted to connect with me and would make funny faces or tease me just to see my smile. At the time, I thought it was because I was a cute kid. I now believe they were responding to the high vibration of my connection to my True Self rather than how I looked.

I was not unique in feeling this abundant connection to my True Self. Many children feel this connection when they are very young, but then start to lose it when the "reality" of the world is taught to us by the adults around us. I lost my connection by the time I was about seven or eight years old. I can remember seemingly out of nowhere feeling very separate and alone. I would work myself into a frenzy at bedtime, wondering to myself, *Who am I? How did I get here? Why am I here? Where will I go when I die?* This self-inquiry lasted for about a year, until the illusion of "reality" became firmly set in my consciousness. I didn't regain this curiosity until I picked up *The Secret* more than three decades later.

I am empathic, which means I am a highly sensitive person who is aware of the emotions and thoughts of others, and I can feel their emotions and thoughts within myself. For most of my life, I didn't know how to deal with these unwanted sensations, and I wasn't aware that often the pain I was feeling wasn't even mine. Left unchecked, picking up on the emotions of everyone took a huge toll on me, and it was a contributing factor to the intensity of my anxiety.

As an empath, I became completely overwhelmed when I was in a public place where there was much negativity or anxiety in the crowd. The energy might be so subtle that a "normal" person might not pick up on it, but for me it was debilitating. I have abruptly left events because the negative energy was just too much for my system to absorb, to the point where I felt intense panic within. This does not go over well when you are accompanied by others who don't feel it and don't want to leave. I have been accused of creating drama by people who cannot understand the real physical overwhelm I feel.

This sensitivity made experiencing the people and events of my childhood even more traumatic. Tantrums would explode from me without warning and there was little anyone could do to console me. These outbursts were the only way I knew how to relieve the pressure that was expanding within me. My family labeled me a spoiled brat, assuming I was looking for ways to garner attention from them. The doctor speculated too much sugar was the culprit. I was banned from having candy until they realized there was no change in my demeanor without it.

None of them realized I was a sponge, absorbing all my family's negative energy into my little body. Not knowing how to positively process this energy, it would bottle up within me until it had nowhere to go but out, like a dam bursting from all the pent-up energy. This happened often, because I was consumed with the energy of my family's pain day in and day out.

I have since learned to embrace the positive side of being empathic and to control the negative side effects. There are so many amazing aspects about having these traits, or superpowers, as I've come to call them. I experience greater intuition, compassion, creativity, and a deeper connection to other people. The benefits of feeling other people's emotions allows me to easily put myself in another's shoes. I can very quickly discern whether someone is being authentic or not. People often come to me for advice, because I can easily align to their feelings on a topic. I also feel more intensely in general; even my positive feelings have greater depth.

By doing life energy work and the exercises I am sharing in this book, I have learned how to deal with the different types of energy I receive from others, and I've come to embrace my sensitivities. Before going to an event, I will check with myself to see if its energy is aligned to mine. If it's not, I just won't go if I don't have to. If I have to attend, I practice presence before, during, and after the event. This keeps me aware of what is happening in my body and mind, helping to discern if negative energy belongs to me or others.

Today, I rarely find myself overwhelmed by the energy of others. When it comes to other people, I trust the feelings in my body to gauge whether their intent with me is positive or negative. I no longer find myself attracting energy vampires – people who subconsciously attach themselves to me to supplement their life energy with my own.

I used this ability to the benefit of others in my career as a technology executive. As a sensitive leader, I am able to better connect and interact with my team members. I can understand their needs and gain perspective from them to deliver results based on the needs of the whole team. As a life energy coach, my empathic abilities help my clients. My ability to sense the state of their energy in my physical body allows me to easily get to the source of the blocks and barriers they need to transform to achieve their desires.

As I learn to wield these superpowers and protect myself from negative energies, I feel far calmer than I ever have in my life. Many people tell me I have an immediate calming effect when I walk into a room, and that the energy changes when I am present. I am now able to bring positive energy to others instead of taking on everyone else's negative emotions and physical pain.

8

CHILDHOOD ADVERSITY

♥

Each of us has events from our past we don't want to share with others for fear of being judged as unworthy. Not one person comes through this life without facing some sort of trauma and pain. I believe we are meant to experience suffering until we know and express our True Self fully. Healing from adversity helps us expand our consciousness into one of love.

I endured many traumatic experiences in my early life, more than most people I know. I couldn't really quantify the expanse of what I experienced until I became aware of The Adverse Childhood Experiences (ACE) Study, conducted in the 1990s by physician researchers Vincent Felitti of Kaiser Permanente and Robert Anda of the U.S. Centers for Disease Control.

The study identified ten adverse childhood experiences that have lasting negative impacts on individuals, including the likelihood of developing anxiety and other unfavorable outcomes to one's health as one grows older. The ten adverse experiences defined by the ACE study are:

1. Physical abuse
2. Sexual abuse
3. Emotional abuse
4. Physical neglect
5. Emotional neglect
6. Mother treated violently
7. Household substance abuse
8. Household mental illness
9. Parental separation or divorce
10. Incarcerated household member

An ACE score of four or more is considered high. I experienced nine of the ten ACEs by the time I was eight years old; no one in my family was ever incarcerated. However, this wasn't the only adversity I had to deal with in my childhood. My family was very poor, I was often bullied by other kids, and my brother almost died of an overdose when he was fourteen years old.

I experienced death in so many other ways at a young age. Both of my parents took their own lives: my dad when I was twelve and my mom when I was seventeen. Two brothers and both my grandfathers died before I was born, my maternal grandma died when I was eight, my dad's sister committed suicide when I was eleven, my paternal grandma died when I was fifteen, and two uncles passed away shortly after I was eighteen.

As a parentless young adult, I learned about life through the school of hard knocks. I struggled for many years financially, facing homelessness when I was eighteen and again at age twenty-one.

Despite all the challenges I endured, my childhood wasn't completely awful. There were some good times and loving moments when I was young, and my family operated as a unit. However, as the years went by, my parents' unhealed emotional pain grew and they alienated themselves from others, pushing themselves deeper into their suffering and pulling us kids with them.

I was born in a small town in Illinois about 100 miles from Chicago. I am the youngest of five children. As I mentioned earlier, two older brothers passed away when they were babies before I was born. My sister, Cheryl, is three years older than me. My half-brother, Bill, is twelve years older, but he always acted much younger than his age thanks to early, hard-core drug use. My mom divorced Bill's dad when he was a small child and married my dad when Bill was eight years old.

My dad was employed at his family's business and my mom didn't work. I will never understand why she stayed home, since we needed the extra money. Instead, she spent most of her days glued to the television, watching game show after game show in the morning before switching to talk programs in the afternoons.

When I was very young, my parents would often socialize with our neighbors, aunts, uncles, and cousins. I had a sense of family and community in my early years. Although we were poor, we still managed to have a few adventures. My mom was a die-hard Chicago Cubs fan and her love for the team was passed on to me. She would hoard pennies for months so we could take a day trip to Wrigley Field to see the Cubs play. Every summer, we had a yard sale, selling our toys to raise the money to go to an amusement park or museum in Chicago.

We took one vacation in my childhood, and it was to visit to my mom's aunt in Nebraska when I was six years old. We drove there in our old station wagon with no air conditioning during the hottest month of summer, sleeping in the car when we stopped at night. It was a boring visit; my mom's aunt and uncle seemed ancient to me, and they lived in a town even smaller than ours. But Cheryl and I were granted a special treat on the way home. Our yard sale that year had proved extra prosperous to us, so my dad diverted to St. Louis to visit the St. Louis Arch and the Six Flags theme park. We arrived in St. Louis in the middle of the night, my dad pulling over to rest in a rough neighborhood. That night I slept with one eye open, partly out of fear of being robbed and partly from the excitement of going to my first big theme park.

On summer weekends we would have cookouts, go bike-riding, or visit our local state parks to picnic and hike. I loved when we would bring charcoal and cookout on one of the park's grills. The hot dogs tasted so much better grilled outside than when we boiled them on the stove at home. Occasionally, we would go camping at one of the local campgrounds for the weekend. My dad would rent a small rowboat so we could fish on the lake. I refused to touch the worms, so he always baited my hook for me. The rare times I actually caught a fish were so exciting to me, but we never kept them. My dad would always throw the fish back into the lake after removing them from the hook.

We weren't allowed to have friends inside our house very often when we were young. They could play in our yard, but my mom would not even allow anyone in to use our bathroom. We could never be certain what state my dad would be in or if there was fighting going on in the house. Some parents wouldn't let their kids play with us at all. At the time, I didn't understand why, and it hurt my feelings by making me think there was something wrong with me. I later realized that my home life wasn't the best environment for any kid to experience.

My dad's drinking was often on public display when he staggered home from one of the local taverns. I was six years old when he came home one Saturday night so drunk that my mom told him he was "in the doghouse." He decided to show her and literally slept outside in our doghouse that night, with only his torso fitting in the small dwelling. The next morning, many people on their way to church saw my dad, passed out on the ground, with his legs hanging outside the doghouse. Needless to say, I lost a few friends after that episode.

Because both my parents were mentally and emotionally unstable, my home life was unpredictable. My parents' illnesses created for me a childhood of instability and constant fear. My dad's alcoholism was paired with deep anger issues. My mom never sought professional help, so she was never diagnosed with a mental illness or personality disorder, but she displayed traits of narcissism, depression, paranoia, insecurity, and anxiety.

My dad spent many weekend afternoons drinking at one of the local bars. When he came home, my siblings and I would quickly assess whether he was going to pass out or start a fight. Personal safety was always on our minds, tension playing in the background even when my dad wasn't around. He was an angry drunk who often beat my mom, my brother, and our three dogs. My sister was next in line and, while it was less common for him to hit me, it did happen. I'd like to think my dad had a soft spot for me given how little I was, but in reality, I think I just got really good at hiding. It was a trait that I carried well into my adult life.

However scary my dad was when he was drunk or angry, nothing compared to the fear I felt when my mom turned on me. Always sober, her words could immediately cut you to your core and rob you of your feelings of self-worth. She could effortlessly turn your positive traits against you. She was the queen of gaslighting, rewriting events and making you lose trust in what you saw and heard from her. She was a consummate victim, blaming everyone else for her circumstances in life.

A master manipulator, my mom relished in playing favorites among us three kids. When you were in her good graces, she gave you positive attention and allowed you special privileges. When you were on her bad side, you were given the silent treatment for days on end, often not knowing what you did to deserve it. She would deny basic care during these periods of silence, leaving us children to fend for ourselves.

My mom was a ruthless gossip, constantly sharing her negative opinions about everyone. She was relentlessly critical and undermining of my dad. Whether he was present or not, she would often complain about how badly he treated her, how poor we were thanks to him, and what a failure he was. She disliked my dad's family and spoke negatively about them all the time. Her sentiments were so personal and full of hate that I felt bad about myself just for being related to them.

As an empath, I became a master at sensing the energy and emotions of everyone I encountered. I had to; for me it was a matter of life or death. Coming home was a scary and stressful proposition. I would put my hand on the front door's doorknob and listen to what was going on in the house, hoping no one inside saw me. If I heard screaming, hitting, dogs barking, and objects being thrown, I had to make a quick choice on whether to go in or not. If I chose to risk it and go inside, I would open the front door very quickly and very quietly. With my heart racing, I quickly assessed the landscape to determine if it was safe to be seen. If the quiet was due to a lull in an ongoing fight, I would bolt as fast as I could to my bedroom, praying that no one noticed me.

When I was too scared to risk going in my house, I wandered around the neighborhood until I felt it might be safe to return. I spent many hours walking around by myself because I was too scared to be at home. While I lived in a climate that was harsh and unpredictable, weather would not stop me from keeping myself safe.

I clearly recall walking by myself in the dark more than once in the winter when I was only seven or eight years old. I felt scared and lonely in the bitter, dark, cold, but I also felt safe. I walked past house after house, the glow of their inside lights shining onto the snow outside. I could see families gathered around their dining tables, laughing and talking while eating dinner together. Lonely, cold, and afraid to go home, I reflected on the story *The Little Match Girl* by Hans Christian Anderson.

The Little Match Girl was poor and all alone, out in the cold trying to sell matchsticks. She was also afraid to go home to her unloving father who would beat her if she didn't sell all the matchsticks. While trying to keep herself warm, she lit the matches and in the flames she saw visions of food, a happy family, a warm stove, and her loving grandmother, who had died.

Fortunately, I did not meet the same as the Little Match Girl, who was found frozen in the snow by passersby the next morning. Instead, for much of my life I carried the pang of loneliness and loss, a grieving that I did not get to be part of a loving and caring family. That loneliness remained with me through most of my adult life.

9

I AM A POWERFUL CREATOR

♥

For a long time after their deaths, I carried much anger toward my parents. At first, I blamed them for everything wrong in my life; later, I acted like they never existed, burying the pain deep within me. When I did talk about my childhood, I didn't dwell on the physical and emotional pain I experienced. Instead, I shrugged it off, touting how strong I was to have endured my childhood and now be functioning so well. While I tried to shove the unresolved pain down deep inside me, it manifested itself in my need to over-control circumstances and it created the anxiety that nearly destroyed me.

As I awakened, I had to heal the energy around my childhood trauma in order to move forward. I learned you can't hide from what happened and life will make you face it, whether you like it or not. As my consciousness developed spiritually, I came to a place of deep gratitude, forgiveness, and understanding for my parents.

This is where the story really begins, what I am here to tell you and teach you. If we were taught this as kids, we would save a lot of heartache and misery for ourselves and for everyone else. However, we are all on different spiritual paths, awakening on our own timing. When we are ready, the messenger appears. If you are reading this book, then you are ready to hear this message.

As I learned in *The Secret*, I am convinced that everything that shows up in your life comes through you. You attract the circumstances in your life through your internal thoughts, beliefs, and feelings. Adversity will keep repeating itself until we heal the root cause and align ourselves to the light within. This is karma.

As infinite beings who reincarnate into this physical plane, we are divine creators of our life experience. We plan our life before we come here, creating circumstances that will help us in all the ways we need to grow in consciousness, and fulfilling the karmic debts from our past lifetimes.

I believe we have held many different lives and our ultimate soul purpose is to know and experience ourselves as the love and divinity we really are, our True Selves. That can mean experiencing a lot of pain, trauma, and heartbreak in our lives to get there. We need to go through these dark trials and tribulations in order to appreciate the essence of who we really are.

Knowing that I planned this life to grow in consciousness, how can I hold my parents in resentment, hate, or anger? I can't. I now have only deep gratitude for them because they were key contributors for me to learn and grow in a big way. The experiences I had with them paved the way for me to heal and expand who I am; to ultimately experience the magnitude of my True Self.

While we defined our life scenario before we were born, we are not stuck with it. We all have free will to act as we want to in this life. When you awaken to your True Self, you learn that you have the power within you to create the life you want. We are all constantly creating, good or bad. When you understand the power of your True Self, you can start creating happiness and joy. As I began to know my True Self, my natural state changed from fear and anxiety to inner peace and calm.

For most of my life, I continually attracted negative experiences because I was living from the level of my anxiety and fears. I was afraid of being criticized, abandoned, hurt, neglected, alone, homeless, and poor. I was afraid to be me. I was afraid of other people. I was afraid of my anxiety. When I started to heal these fears, I no longer experienced them in my life. Instead, I began to attract positive and loving experiences.

I stopped feeling like a victim and started appreciating the circumstances of my life. I held myself accountable for my actions and began to take responsibility to recreate my life from a higher consciousness. I began to live from my True Self, with love as the basis for my actions. I took control of my personal life energy in order to attract experiences and people that match love, the essence of my True Self.

You can do this, too. I challenge you to ask yourself, "How do I want to be in this world? Do I want to be a victim who is manipulated from the outside? Or a powerful creator from within?"

10

LIFE WITH DAD

♥

Like most little girls, I had a special place in my heart for my dad. To me, he was larger than life. He seemed so tall when I was little, like a giant, but he was only 5'8". I loved it when he would sit me on his lap and play "Got Your Nose," pretending to take my nose off my face and hiding it from me. I laughed and laughed as I tried to get my nose back. I felt so happy when he would throw me in the air, singing a song my family had made up about my googly-eyes. He had blue-ink tattoos on his arms that I loved to trace with my little fingers when I was sitting on his lap. One of my very favorite photos is of me when I was about three years old, curled up and sleeping in his arms.

My dad was a gearhead, spending much of his free time in the driveway tinkering with whatever old car he had at the time. A cabinetmaker by trade, he crafted many items out of wood such as a dollhouse for me, a fenced dog enclosure for the yard, and a cutout of Santa that we displayed on our porch every Christmas season. He fancied himself a handyman, tackling various do-it-yourself projects around the house. I loved hanging around his workspace, helping him out or playing with his tools. We never spoke much but there was always a comfortable silence, a camaraderie, between the two of us.

Unfortunately, I was never sure when I could have those peaceful moments with my dad. His mood depended on whether he was sober or drunk. When I was very little, his state of being was hard for me to decipher but I learned to quickly read his behavior as I grew up. When I realized he was drunk, I would remove myself from his presence as quickly and quietly as I could.

I now understand why my dad was the way he was. He had his own demons to deal with and this was how he chose to cope. While his mother was a loving woman, his dad was a whole different story. I never met my grandpa because he died before I was born, but the stories I heard of him tell of a viciously mean drunk, a cruel man far more abusive than my dad ever was.

I learned at a very young age that I couldn't let people see me. I had to hide in my own home, the place that should be a sanctuary for every child. To avoid the emotional and physical abuse from my parents, I became adept at making myself instantly invisible as much as possible. It was only when they didn't see me that I could be safe from them.

One day when I was six years old, it was an abnormally quiet Sunday afternoon in our house. I was playing with my Barbie dolls alone upstairs in the bedroom I shared with my sister. My dad was across the street at the tavern, his favorite hangout. My mom was lying on the couch in the living room watching TV, her favorite pastime. My brother and sister were at my maternal grandma's house for the afternoon.

My dad came home earlier than expected, probably because he had spent all the money from his last paycheck. He was drunk and angry. Right away, a fight between my parents broke out and I could hear my dad start to hit my mom. She started screaming as he became more forceful. I remember clearly to this day how my little heart was pounding while the fear grew within me. My thoughts raced back and forth between wondering if my mom was going to die or if he would come looking for me next. All I knew is that I could not let him find me. No way.

This was the first time I remember not having my brother or sister there to protect me. I was on my own and I looked frantically around the room for a hiding spot. There were not many options, since my sister and I didn't have a closet in our room. My parents were downstairs, right below me. I couldn't risk making the slightest noise that would make my father come upstairs to investigate. I very quietly and slowly grabbed BunBun, my favorite stuffed bunny, and slid under the bed. My heart was beating so loud I was afraid he could hear it through the thin floor!

As the fighting grew more violent, I realized my only chance for safety was to get out of the house. When the hitting and the screaming halted for a few minutes, I mustered up my courage, slid out from under the bed, and ran down the stairs as swiftly as I could. I bolted through the dining room and past the doorway of the living room where I could see my dad looming threateningly over my mom. I picked up speed as I ran through the kitchen to the back door, pushing open the screen door and letting it slam behind me. I never looked back, pumping my skinny little legs as hard as they would go until I reached my grandma's house, seven blocks away.

What a sight I must have made running down the street! When I got to my grandma's I was panting, hanging on to BunBun for dear life, and covered from head-to-toe in dust-bunnies that I had collected while lying under my bed. My grandma was not happy to see me in this state and she clucked her disapproval when I told her about the situation at home. She did not like my dad and preferred to stay far away from him, but now I had put her in the position to rescue her youngest daughter from his abuse. I don't remember what happened next except that my mom ended up in the hospital with broken ribs.

Yet my mom stayed with my dad and the fighting continued, growing more violent with each incident. When I was eight years old, after one extremely intense night of abuse, my parents decided to divorce. My brother, sister, and I were to stay with my mom and there was no set schedule to see my dad. I missed him during that time. He had moved in with his mom and I would walk the mile to her house as often as I could. Sometimes, he took me and my sister out shopping, but otherwise we rarely saw him.

As much as I felt the emptiness of not having my dad at home, it was a relief to not have to worry about the fighting. I could easily walk in the door without thinking about my physical safety. During that time, my mom left me alone for the most part. I was caught up in playing with my friends and our new collie-husky puppy, Sparkle, whom my parents let me get when they were still together. This was also the time my mom and sister started spending more time with each other. They were often out and about while I stayed home with my brother.

Unfortunately, this time of peace was short-lived. When I was nine years old, my parents decided to re-wed. They were very matter of fact when they told me the news.

I hesitated before responding, because I didn't want to live with the fighting again. Seeing their expectant looks, I told them I was happy about it. After all, there was a part of me that did miss the sober version of my dad and having a car to go places. My mom didn't have her driver's license, so we usually had to walk everywhere we needed to go. Occasionally, she would ask a friend for a ride or hire a cab to take us places not within walking distance.

The fighting resumed almost as soon as my dad moved back in. It quickly escalated, becoming more frequent, more brutal, and lasting longer than before. My mom once again ended up in the hospital after my dad choked her in one particularly violent episode.

After that, she would escape him by coming into my room to sleep in my bed with me on the nights he was out drinking. She knew it was unlikely my dad would come after her in my room. Once in my bed, she slept peacefully, snoring deeply throughout the night. I did not get much sleep on those nights as I absorbed my mom's fearful energy into my little body. This negative energy made it near impossible for me to settle down and relax. I went to school many days with huge bags under my eyes, struggling to stay awake during class.

My dad was a master at promising the moon, but he rarely delivered. Even simple promises like getting ice cream, giving us a ride to meet our friends, or buying the clothes we desperately needed didn't manifest. How could he follow through when much of the time he was either drunk or passed out?

My dad got a perverse thrill in making us beg him for the things we needed or wanted. Small things, big things, it didn't matter. He would egg us on and have us pleading for hours, to the point where we felt anxious desperation for our desires. He seemed to get a strange satisfaction out of extending our longing. Sometimes he gave in to our requests, but often he would get sick of the game and just tell us no.

As a child, I became cynical of the intentions of others. I grew to expect nothing from people, no matter who they were and what they promised. But as I expanded my consciousness, I learned that the source of all things comes through our True Self, not other people. If we are aligned energetically to what we want and what we need, it will come to us. We may not be able to dictate exactly how or from whom, but we can trust that all our needs are met. Later in this book, I will share True-Self exercises that can help you align your life energy to the outcomes you desire.

11

BOUNDARIES

Having healthy boundaries with others, both physical and emotional, is important for everyone, especially children. In developing a sense of self, a child should be allowed to have control over their own body. They must be able to exercise the right to say no when someone does something they do not like or puts them in harm's way. In my childhood, I was not able to exercise control over my body thanks to three important men in my life: my dad, my brother, and my uncle.

My dad was a sore loser about everything, even when he played board games with his own children. Losing a game of Monopoly could result in him throwing chairs and upending the kitchen table while he swore at us, his face red with anger. On other occasions, in the spirit of "fun", he would tease me and Cheryl unmercifully, often bringing us to tears. Our crying triggered anger in our dad to the point where he would tell us to stop or we would get the belt. His reaction was unpredictable. Whether or not we got the belt depended more on his mood than our ability to stop crying.

My dad took extreme pleasure in exploiting our weaknesses. He knew I was deathly afraid of heights but twice talked me into going on elevated amusement park rides, telling me he would keep me safe. The first time happened we went on the cable car ride at Six Flags in St. Louis when I was six years old.

The ride unexpectedly stopped at its highest point, 100 feet above the ground, leaving me terrified, clinging to the side of the car. My dad began shaking the car until it was furiously swinging back and forth. He laughed at my tears and screams, telling me the ride was stuck and I would have to climb down a firetruck ladder to safety. My mom laughed along with him, almost egging him on.

My fear turned to panic just as the ride started up again a few minutes later and completed without a hitch. Still crying, I felt indescribable relief when my feet were back on solid ground.

The next time occurred when my dad convinced me to go on the double Ferris wheel at the local carnival when I was eight years old. I was in awe and terrified of how high the top wheel reached but I wanted to be brave, so I gave it a shot.

When our wheel was the bottom one, it wasn't so bad, and I began to relax, enjoying the view as the wheel circled. However, when the wheels shifted and we ascended to the top, my dad began rocking our car back and forth so hard it felt like we were going to tip out of it.

Like the cable car ride, my tears and pleas to stop only spurred him on. He continued to rock the car while making fun of my fear. He stopped only when we were once again the bottom wheel, and other people could witness his actions.

For a long time after that experience, I stuck to amusement rides that stayed close to the ground. The fear of heights remains deep to this day, although there are activities that no longer scare me, such as flying in a plane.

Another weakness I have is being extremely ticklish. My dad would get a kick out of tickling me to hear me laugh. At first it was fun, because I really liked to get positive attention from him. However, the fun would quickly turn to torture for me. When you are sensitive to tickling, the sensations in your body can easily turn from pleasure to pain. My dad would keep tickling me even when my laughter turned to desperate pleas to stop. Instead, he would turn up the intensity of his actions.

Inevitably, I couldn't take the torture any longer and I would start crying, begging for my mom to come help me. She chose not to intervene out of fear that my dad would turn his negative attention toward her. The tickling episodes almost always ended with him being angry at me for spoiling his idea of fun. He would show his disdain for my weakness by either smacking me across the face or pushing me away in disdain while swearing at me.

My brother, Bill, also took great delight in tickling me. Taking cues from my dad, he also would not stop when I begged him to. My mom would tell Bill to stop, if she was aware of what was happening. If she was not home, I had no choice but to endure the tickling until he tired of it. Bill especially delighted in putting a pillow on my face, sitting on it, and farting while he tickled me.

Bill would often terrorize Cheryl and me when he babysat us, chasing us into the bathroom and threatening harm if we dared to come out. We spent hours locked in the bathroom to stay safe, waiting for our parents to come home. Bill would let us out only when he heard my dad's car pull up in the driveway. Cheryl and I would rush to tell our mom what had transpired while they were gone.

Bill always denied any role in wrongdoing, and she would punish Cheryl and me for tattling on him.

It is not uncommon for siblings to antagonize each other, but Bill was twelve years older than me and he was an adult when he behaved like this, not another child. I grew up leery of all adult men in my life.

Our parents often put me and my siblings in situations that jeopardized our safety. One such situation occurred one fall afternoon when I was eight years old, and Cheryl and I were home alone with our dad.

The house we were living in at the time was very old and had an unfinished cellar that you entered through a door on the side of the house. The small space was creepy, with cinder block walls and a heavy, dank smell. It was full of dusty clutter, mostly useless items left by past inhabitants over the years. All sorts of bugs scurried back and forth on the floor and up the walls. The room had a couple of small windows and there was one light hanging from the ceiling, but the bulb was burned out.

Cheryl and I were playing in our bedroom when our dad ordered us to get our coats on and go outside. It was getting late and the sun was beginning to go down. He brought us to the cellar, opened its weather-beaten door, and ordered us to go down the stairs. Terrified, Cheryl and I begged him not to make us go in there. Ignoring our pleas, he forced us down the stairs and slammed the door on us, locking us in from the outside.

We heard our dad start up the car and pull away. Terrified, Cheryl and I sat huddled together in the cramped space as darkness fell; the only light we could see was from the streetlamp outside the house. We passed the time making up stories and singing songs, wishing that our mom would return home to let us out.

After a couple of hours, we heard our dad's car return. We were dismayed when we heard him go into the house, his footsteps creaking on the floorboards above our heads. He must have remembered that he had put us in the cellar because he soon came to fetch us. He was so drunk he could barely walk straight. Cheryl and I ran quickly past him into the house and locked ourselves in the bedroom we shared.

He didn't come looking for us though, instead he passed out almost immediately in his chair in the living room. We waited impatiently in our room for our mom to come back. I don't recall her reaction to what had transpired, only that Cheryl and I felt much safer with her presence at home.

Another situation where my boundaries were violated occurred on a regular basis. My dad's mom didn't drive, so my dad often would take her to the grocery store or out for other errands. My mom would go with them, but they wouldn't take me and Cheryl. There wasn't enough room in the car for all of us and we were a distraction to the tasks at hand. If Bill was not home to babysit us, we would be left at our grandma's house with my dad's brother to watch us for the few hours they would be gone.

I don't remember when my uncle first started to abuse me and Cheryl, but I was definitely too young to understand what was going on. Shortly after my parents and grandma left the house, he would start touching us in an inappropriate manner. We would try to not get close to him, but he was much bigger and stronger than we were.

He would grab one of us as we tried to get away, pulling us up to his overweight body. I remember trying to push him away and pry his arms off of me with all my might, but I was no match for him. It was the worst thing I've ever experienced in my life. Fully clothed and smelling like pipe smoke, he would rub his crotch up against me, forcing me to stand there as his movements became more intense. And then just like that, it would be over, and he would mostly ignore me and Cheryl for the rest of the time we were there.

I look back today and wonder what my parents were thinking by leaving us two young girls alone with our uncle. He was mentally disabled, and was like a big kid, not much more mature than we were. Cheryl and I repeatedly begged our mom to please not leave us alone with him. We told her what he did to us and that we didn't like it. She responded that we had no choice but to go, and that we should try harder to avoid him. She ordered us to not say anything to our dad and they continued to leave us with our uncle.

When Cheryl and I were older, my mom told us that he had been criminally charged for molesting a young girl years before. I do not know whether that statement is true or if it was one of the stories she would make up about others. Either way, to this day it shocks me that two young girls would be left alone with him.

I'm not sure what would have transpired if my dad knew what was happening. He wasn't one to stand up to his family and I'm not sure he would have believed me and Cheryl. She and I felt so helpless, both with the situation and that we had no choice but to comply with our mom's commands. I started to blame myself for my uncle's actions, thinking that if only I could move faster to get away from him, I could stop him from attacking me.

I believe my mom ignored our pleas for her own selfish reasons – she didn't want my dad and grandma to be alone without her. She always felt that my grandma made most of the decisions related to our family. Forcing herself on them might give my mom a chance to influence the outcome. I can certainly understand that she wanted to have control over what happened in her marriage and family life. What I will never understand is why our mom continued to put me and Cheryl in direct contact with our uncle, knowing what he was doing to us.

After my parents divorced when I was eight years old, my mom no longer went shopping with my dad and grandma. Our uncle never babysat us again. After my parents remarried when I was nine years old, my mom said we were old enough to stay home by ourselves. Cheryl was twelve years old and very mature, so it made sense for her to be alone. Given my young age, I now wonder if this was my mom's way of protecting me from my uncle, but I will never know.

Only a child who was molested by an adult can understand the sense of deep shame that comes with the abuse; your feelings of self-worth wither away each time you are violated. When I was a child, I didn't understand exactly what my uncle was doing or why he was doing it, but I knew it was wrong. I felt ashamed of myself that I wasn't strong enough to stop him and later, many years after his death, I still felt anger at him for stealing a big part of my innocence from me. My mom's lack of response to me and Cheryl's pleas to shield us from him only accelerated my dwindling sense of self-worth.

It took decades for me to heal from the abuses by the men in my family and to get to a place where I can let someone touch me without going into fight-or-flight mode. Trusting others with my body did not come easily for me, no matter how innocent or normal the act. After healing the trauma related to the events I shared in this chapter, I can now completely relax with others when I know the intention is loving. However, I still go to my old defenses if someone ignores my boundaries and tries to touch me when I say no.

12

YOUR MIND IS AN AMAZING STORYTELLER

———— ♥ ————

To know your True Self, you need to understand who you are not. Most people associate themselves with their thoughts, which come from the Ego Mind. After all, this is where the sense of who we are comes from, right? The Ego Mind would certainly like to have you believe it's who you are, but this is not your True Self. Our Ego Mind is not where our true power lies. It knows that, but it doesn't want you to figure it out. Once you know where your power comes from you will no longer allow the Ego Mind to rule you.

The mind itself is an amazingly useful tool that takes in information from outside of us and helps us make sense of the physical world. We need our minds to exist on this planet. The Ego Mind, however, takes in all the impressions, beliefs, and experiences we encountered since we were young children and uses them to create an image of ourselves and the external world. Much of this information comes from other's beliefs, most of which are negative and limiting. For many of us, the resulting images are critical and judgmental, with a sense of separation from all else around us.

When asked "Who are you?" my Ego Mind might answer "I am a mother, sister, VP, runner, life energy coach, dog lover, and author." But these are really just attributes that may change over time. We grow up believing that the image that lives in our mind is who we are. It is not. We are separate from our minds.

There is the presence within you that is your True Self and then there is your False Self, constructed by your Ego Mind. Your True Self is the steady light within you, the constant consciousness that, for most of us, has taken a back seat to the Ego Mind. I believe that knowing our True Self means overcoming the Ego Mind that is running our lives.

The Ego Mind plays a big part in creating our life experiences. The beliefs, thoughts, and feelings generated from the content of it, most of it held in our subconscious mind, attract to us people and situations that match it. If your beliefs are negative, your life experience will include a never-ending cycle of non-loving events. That is, until you can break the pattern and replace the adverse stories and feelings with positive, loving ones.

Limiting beliefs keep you from creating the world you really want to experience. Most limiting beliefs are based in fear and lack. We all carry limiting beliefs we've held since our childhood that we learned from our parents, teachers, and others. Our most formative years are from conception to age seven. This is when our beliefs of the world get set in our Ego Mind about who we really are, what our worth is, and what we expect to happen to us.

What is a limiting belief? It is a belief that has boundaries around it, such as:

I will never be rich.
Only rich people can make money.
It's hard to make money.
I get sick every January.
Poor health runs in my family.
It's impossible to lose weight and keep it off.
Girls are not as good as boys at math.
I am old.
You can't trust anyone in this world.
A woman can't do the job as well as a man.

Your beliefs, both good and bad, set your future up to be a repeat of the past, proving that your "reality" is right. Limiting beliefs keep you from growing as a person. We are aware of many limiting beliefs that are within our consciousness but there are even more that are hidden, buried deep within our subconscious. Ask yourself if you have any limiting beliefs. First, your Ego Mind will trick you and say you don't. Ego Minds are like that. They're always right, they want to keep us safe, and they judge everything we do.

Because of my early childhood experiences, my most limiting belief was that every person on this planet was a threat to my safety. I lived in constant fear of others. This contributed to the deep anxiety I felt all the time, in all my relationships, and in my daily interactions with others. Since life really is only about interacting with others, you can imagine that my life wasn't showing up so great for me. If we think everyone is out to get us, metaphorically speaking, we will build walls around us to keep the bad guys out and use our own internal weapons to defend against these perceived threats.

Life reflects back to us what is in our beliefs. People are good. People are bad. It's really your choice in what you think. Albert Einstein summed it up perfectly when he said, "I think the most important question facing humanity is, 'Is the universe a friendly place?' This is the first and most basic question all people must answer for themselves."

For most of my life, the answer to this question would have been a fast and firm "No." As I grew in my consciousness, I knew the Universe would be what I believed it to be and that I needed to change my limiting beliefs to have it show up like I wanted it to. Today, I answer Einstein's question with a resounding, "Yes!"

As an adult, the many limiting beliefs I held created so much anxiety for me. I was not moving forward with what I wanted to do in my life, and my self-talk was keeping me stuck exactly where I was. Yet I was "safe" because I wasn't putting myself out there; I was sticking with the status quo.

My limiting beliefs came from my parents, siblings, teachers, peers, the news, magazines, movies, and TV shows. I had also developed a very strong ego consciousness due to my need to focus on my personal safety when I was a child. I was besieged with limiting beliefs, and everything I attracted into my experience confirmed these adverse views.

My Ego Mind was fearful, anxious, judgmental, hyper-critical, separate, and untrusting toward myself and almost everyone else. It created lengthy, detailed stories of lack and limitation. It used fear to "keep me safe" but it really just created a world on an endless repetition of these limits. I continued to attract experiences that matched my Ego Mind when I left it to run on autopilot. My Ego

YOUR MIND IS AN AMAZING STORYTELLER

Mind often said things to me like: "Who do you think you are," "You can't do anything right," and "No one will ever love you." It's very easy to fall in the Ego Mind's trap, as it seduces you into unconsciousness about who you are.

I feel my parents' behaviors were created by not having control over their Ego Minds. Their deep belief in its negative stories ultimately led to their suicides. My dad had probably also developed a strong ego consciousness from the abuse he suffered as a child at the hands of his father. My mom's acts of constant criticism and talking poorly about everyone were driven by her Ego Mind. She sequestered herself from others with no positive input coming in to dispute it, allowing her Ego Mind to run rampant on its negative course. The Ego Mind loves to feed on negativity, and my mom's mind was a fertile place for it.

You can step back and watch your Ego Mind using the exercises in this book. When you do, you will be amazed at what your mind can come up with. It will take one thought and then another until before you know it, you have spiraled into a deep sea of negativity. Left unchecked, you will attract life experiences that match the negative vibration of the feelings behind the thoughts.

As I watch my Ego Mind, I find that what it comes up with can be outrageous and fantastical sometimes, while purely frightening at other times. The Ego Mind loves to be the victim and it can be truly comical to observe how easily offended it can become at another person's innocent actions. It is so smooth that you don't even realize you have been lured down this destructive path. The Ego Mind is addicted to low-vibration thoughts and loves to wallow in them, endlessly multiplying them while creating deep suffering for you. The Ego Mind will not relent until you stop it. If you don't, you will be overcome by stress, anxiety, depression, and, in its worst form, suicidal thoughts.

When I started nurturing the light within and healing the limiting beliefs that were in my Ego Mind, my life began to drastically change. Getting out of my head and focusing on my heart allowed me to create a world that better reflected my True Self. You can also change by living from your True Self. With practice, you will begin to see your Ego Mind as a partner in the expansion of your consciousness.

As I connect more to the light within me, I become aware of how my Ego Mind operates. I can clearly see the limiting thoughts and judgments it brings to almost every situation. Instead of wallowing in them, I now see they are extremely valuable in showing me where I am out of alignment with my True Self. I can use this awareness to heal my disconnection from who I really am. The more I heal, the stronger my light begins to shine, and I come closer to living fully from this divine space. I can begin to bring in love to all circumstances. From here, I create a new cycle of attracting amazing and loving experiences into my life experience.

If you regularly practice the exercises in this book, you will learn to observe your negative thoughts without attaching to them. You can consciously replace them by using powerful, loving affirmations, and you will start to experience a whole new reality.

Much of the world we live in today has been driven by the Ego Mind, with tragic results. The endless wars, high crime, mass shootings, discrimination, separation, and mainstream media manipulation are all symptoms of the selfish, separate Ego Mind.

I believe if everyone were able to become observers of their Ego Minds and detach from its destructive messages, we could all start to live from our True Selves. Together, we could shift the vibration of this planet from one of fear, judgment, separation, and lack to one of love, acceptance, togetherness, and abundance. We could begin to live heaven on earth.

13

TRUE-SELF EXERCISE

♥

Limiting beliefs often result in stuck energy within our body, showing up as feelings that alert us to where we are not aligned with love. These low-vibrational feelings may include fear, guilt, anger, avoidance, and shame. The blocked energy may manifest as anxiety, pain, illness, or disease. Without providing a healthy outlet, the negative feelings will accumulate and remain bottled within us for our lifetime.

We all have limiting beliefs about ourselves and the world around us. As I described in the last chapter, limiting beliefs control what we think is possible. They directly impact what we will experience in our lives. More examples of common limiting beliefs include:

I am a failure.
I don't deserve to have anything better.
No one will ever love me for who I am.
Other people are more important than I am.
I will never have enough money to do what I want to do.
I am too old to (fill in the blank).
You can't be rich doing the work you love.

In this section, I will show you how to relieve stuck energy from your body by using the Release Technique. Doing this technique will help you to identify and clear limiting beliefs from your mind and body. When you do this work on a regular basis, you will begin to loosen the feelings of anxiety and stress you carry around every day.

You will become closer to your True Self. You will be able to transcend the fears and the limiting beliefs that have kept you in an unfulfilling existence. When you become clear and calm, you will more quickly manifest the life you desire. You will begin to embody the power of your True Self.

Method: Release Technique

The Release Technique will help you clear negative energy from your body. This technique aids in identifying limiting beliefs, which will appear as you put your focus within your body. Limiting beliefs will come to the surface when you give undivided attention to yourself. You will learn to appreciate the power of the body-mind-spirit connection.

You can do this process while focused on a limiting belief or just focus on where you feel discomfort in your body. This discomfort may show up as pain, illness, anxiety, or other unhelpful feelings. You should repeat the Release Technique often to keep your body clear of negative energy.

The first time you do this exercise, it's important to put your full focus on the sensations within your body. Therefore, I recommend going to a place where you won't be disturbed. Get comfortable in the best way for you, it doesn't matter if you are standing, sitting, or lying down.

How to Practice the Release Technique:

1. Begin with the "Connect to Your Heart Space" exercise.
2. Once you feel you have connected to your heart space, picture a brilliant golden light coming down from about two feet above your head. As you breathe in, picture this light coming in through the crown of your head and filling your entire body.
3. Take a few more deep breaths. Focus within your body and identify where you are feeling pain or distress. Keeping your attention on this area, continue to breathe.
4. As thoughts come up, observe them but don't attach to them. Let them go.
5. Keep breathing until the feeling has lessened or you can no longer feel it. Your body may start to feel looser, calmer, and sometimes you will feel joy within.
6. The feelings of pain or distress may shift to other parts of your body. Move your focus to them and repeat steps 4 and 5.
7. You may not be able to fully release negativity or pain in a single session. This is completely normal. However, every time you focus on an area in your body, you are moving toward fully releasing the negative energy.
8. Once you are finished, return your attention to your heart space and take a few deep, calming breaths.
9. After completing the Release Technique, it is very important to send love to yourself. Often the person you most need to love is yourself! We are

hardest on ourselves and judge our own actions more harshly than anyone else does. We are often our own worst critic. Sending love *and* forgiving ourselves helps us clear our energetic body to attract what we want into our lives.

While focused on your heart space, say to yourself:

> "I see myself as my True Self only. I am pure love, perfect in every way. I am thankful for all the gifts my suffering has brought to me and for the healing that is now under way. I forgive myself. I bless myself, and I celebrate myself. I love myself!"

10. You may want to journal about what came up during your session. Record any limiting beliefs that came into your awareness. Notice how you feel about them now. If you are no longer triggered, celebrate! If you do feel resistance to the limiting belief, I recommend focusing on it during your next Release Technique session.

Healing Symptoms

When you move or transform negative energy, you may experience various healing symptoms immediately or up to several days after doing the Release Technique or other energy methods. These may include:

- During the exercise, you may start yawning, burping, sneezing, passing gas, or having other reactions in your body. Don't be embarrassed.

- Instead celebrate that you are clearing low-frequency energetic gunk from your system.
- You may feel more agitated or anxious than usual as the low vibration energy moves from your being. Recognize this and do not react to the intense feelings, as they should clear over the next few days.
- Your body may go into detox mode after a significant clearing. You may feel exhausted and have the desire to sleep for a couple of days. You might also develop cold or flu-like symptoms. After one intense clearing session around a rocky relationship with my boss, I ended up extremely sick for four days. The detoxification was so intense I couldn't even get out of bed. However, it was well worth it because my relationship with my boss was miraculously harmonious once I returned to work.

Remedies

- Drink lots of water before, during, and after doing the exercises in this book.
- Get up and move! Put on your favorite music and dance. Go outside for a walk. Do yoga. Do whatever it is that gets your energy moving as long as it's low impact. Moving energy takes energy, so running, weightlifting, or playing a sport might fatigue you and bring about more severe symptoms.
- Avoid alcohol.

TRUE-SELF EXERCISE

- Take an Epsom-salt bath and add a few drops of a high-quality essential oil, such as lavender, rose, eucalyptus, or tea-tree oil.
- Go easy on yourself! Let go of expectations and have fun watching the new, positive experiences that come up for you.

14

SHINE YOUR LIGHT

♥

As I reconnect to my True Self, I am reclaiming the light that shone so brightly when I was a young child. The light faded quickly as each year of my childhood went by. My family members did everything they could to dim it. I was a very active child with a high metabolism, constantly looking for outlets for all the energy within myself. My high energy drove my parents nuts, since it didn't align with their state of depression and inactivity. They often said to me things like:

> "Goddammit, Amy, can you just sit still? You are so annoying!"
> "Shut up, Amy, you are giving me a goddamn headache."
> "Stop singing, Amy, your voice sounds like shit."
> "Dammit, Amy, can you just go somewhere else? You are getting on my nerves."

Being empathic, the energy within my body was not all mine. I didn't know how to control it. It was strong and nearly impossible to contain. Thus, I couldn't always control my actions. If I continued to move around or express myself, I could get on my dad's final nerve and he would soon threaten to bring out the belt. Well, no one wants to feel the belt on their bottom, especially a small child, so I stopped expressing myself at home as much as I could.

This was the start of hiding myself, which only became more pronounced as I progressed through school. I did well and I loved to learn. Most subjects came easily to me, especially Math and English. In fact, I loved school so much that one of my favorite pastimes was to play school, either alone or with friends.

When I was nine years old, my dad created a play schoolroom for me in a corner of the basement in our new house. On one of his trips to the junkyard, my dad salvaged a couple of old schoolroom desks and the top of a ping-pong table that he mounted on the wall as a makeshift chalkboard. Even though the room was dank and dark, I spent hours in the basement, joyfully pretending I was a teacher. When my friends came over, we would take turns being teacher or student. When I was alone, I would sit my stuffed animals in the seats and lecture them on Math and English topics.

It was at this time I began going to a much smaller school. Its curriculum was behind that of my prior school, and I had already completed the material that was being taught in the new class. I was bored most of the time but made high grades, and the teachers liked me. To most of the other kids, I was the teacher's pet. I didn't try to be or even want it. I loved learning with all my heart and the teachers responded to my enthusiasm.

At the end of every school year, an award ceremony was held recognizing the students for their academic and athletic accomplishments. In the fifth grade, I received an honor roll pin for achieving straight As and trophies for volleyball, cheerleading, and track. When it came time to present the Super Student of the Year award, I was shocked when I heard my teacher call my name. I was so self-conscious going up to receive the trophy but, on the inside, I was excited at being acknowledged for my accomplishments.

Cheryl also excelled in school and had been well rewarded that day, too. Knowing we were going to be recognized, my parents made a rare appearance at the school that day. We met them at the end of the ceremony so they could take our awards home. While Cheryl and I went on the school picnic, my parents took the medals and trophies to the local diner so they could brag to the other patrons about how smart their daughters were.

My classmates were not at all excited about me receiving the Super Student award and several told me exactly how undeserving they thought I was. No one talked to me during the picnic, including my friends. I spent the whole event feeling super sad, as if I didn't belong. I clung by my teacher's side the entire time. Not only did I get the silent treatment at home, I was now experiencing it with my friends.

I came home in tears, crying to my mom about what had happened. Her advice? Don't try so hard and you will have friends. "But I wasn't even trying!" I cried to her, feeling immediately how unfair her advice was.

I was already trying to blend in with the class and downplay my abilities when I really wanted to excel and learn. Even before the silent treatment at the school picnic, I was made fun of and bullied for the good grades I received. On test days, I was often the first to finish the material, but I didn't want to be seen as the first to hand in the completed work. Not wanting to draw attention to myself, I would sit at my desk and check my answers once, then twice, then often a third time, waiting for someone else to get up and hand their test in first.

My situation fell on my mom's deaf ears and she told me, "Maybe if you weren't so smart, people would like you."

Even as a child, I was stunned by my mom's advice. I already learned that I needed to hide at home to stay safe. Now, my own mother was telling me to diminish who I was, the part of me that came so easily and naturally, so other people would like me. She repeated this message often to me over the years, pushing me to hide who I was even more. I was afraid to be myself except with my closest friends. The "shy" label was often used to describe me. In reality, I was scared to death to be myself!

Not knowing what else to do, and partly because I thought it would please her, I listened to my mom's advice. I went from being a straight-A student in the fifth grade to getting a mix of A's and B's in the sixth grade. I remember consciously selecting wrong answers on tests to get a lower grade and fit in more with my peers. Did I have more friends? Probably not, but I definitely did not receive as much bullying about my grades from the sixth grade onward.

The fear of standing out stayed with me long into adulthood, affecting my professional career and my personal relationships. For many years, I hid my life from others, wanting so much to "blend in" and be "normal." I didn't want people to find out what I had gone through in my childhood. I didn't want to stand out for the adversity I had experienced, what I thought might make me appear defective or less than others. It seemed so unfair that I had to go through so much to get to what I perceived as the normal starting point for everyone else.

I have since learned that there is no "normal" or "easy" baseline for humanity. On different paths through many lifetimes, we all experience what we need to, when we need it. So many people are suffering in this world. In my circles, people had suffered and were continuing to suffer, just in different ways than I had.

There is no measure to suffering. While I have faced so much trauma in my life, there are people who are experiencing much more. While others have not experienced as many tragic events as me, just one loss or one traumatic situation can create a lifetime of suffering. My hope is that my story will help those who are seeking peace from their pain to see they can discover their True Self. To know they can create a life that is loving, joyful, and what they truly deserve. We all deserve this.

I now know my journey of being repressed before finding my way back to my True Self is my path to my life purpose. The light within me is burning so strong with the desire to share my story with the world, knowing that it will help others see the light and strength we all have within us. This is the true power of who we are.

15

LIFE WITH MOM

———— ♥ ————

While my relationship with my dad was rocky at best, my relationship with my mom was the hardest and scariest for me. She didn't drink and she didn't physically abuse us. Instead, she was mentally and emotionally unstable, playing narcissistic mind games and using insults to gain control. When in one of her moods, she could instantly diminish my sense of self with only a few well-chosen words, or she would give me the silent treatment that could last for days. I was never certain which version of my mom I was interacting with, because her personality could instantly shift from pleasant to mean during the course of a single conversation.

When I was very young, I was very attached to my mom and I would experience deep separation anxiety when she would leave the house. My parents had to sneak out while my older brother and sister would try to distract me from seeing they were leaving. When I realized they were not in the house, I would immediately panic and run to the dining room window which faced our driveway. I would pull myself up on the windowsill, frantically trying to lift myself high enough to see if the car was still in the driveway, tears streaming down my face.

While she wasn't physically abusive like my dad, there was one way my mom liked to cause physical distress for me. She did not wash my hair in the bath, preferring instead to use the kitchen sink. She would lay my body across the kitchen counter, positioning me face down with my head under the water faucet. Staring at the drain, the anticipation alone of what was to come caused me to panic and I would fight to get away.

My mom held me firmly while the water and shampoo streamed down the back of my head and into my ears, before running into my eyes, nose, and mouth. I couldn't see, hear, or breathe as the water overtook my senses. I cried and choked on the water, pleading for her to stop.

My fighting angered my mom, causing her pace to slow as she struggled with my wriggling body. My hair extended to the middle of my back, and it took a long time for her to finish. Finally, when I was five years old, she had all my hair cut off. While I was sad to lose my long, golden hair, I was happy at the freedom I gained. I was now able to wash my hair on my own and no longer had to endure her terrifying shampoos.

When my mom sent me and Cheryl to swimming lessons at the public pool, I was kicked out on the very first day. I was terrified to put my face in the water and to feel it move into my eyes, nose, and ears. The teenage instructors were impatient with me and yelled at me repeatedly to do the bobs with the other kids. I stubbornly refused and they forced me to leave before the lesson was over. I walked out alone feeling humiliated and like a failure, but I also was relieved to be safe from the water. My mom was not happy that I didn't complete the lesson, but she didn't make me return. She hadn't learned to swim herself and didn't put much importance in it.

To this day, I suffer a deep fear of water. I took swimming lessons as an adult and learned to manage the fear during different periods of my life, enabling myself to enjoy water-skiing, snorkeling, surfing, and paddle boarding. It's only been in the last ten years that I could take a shower and comfortably let the water hit my face. If I don't keep my water skills up to date, I can easily sink back into this fear. This is a deep trauma for which I still need to do more work and use the power of my True Self to help me heal!

My mom regularly played favorites among us three kids, using the silent treatment to let you know when you were the unfavored one. There was rarely a logical reason for being put on her bad side, leaving us kids to try to figure out why our own mother wouldn't talk to us.

I remember leaving for school in the morning with everything normal – as normal as it could be in our house – and coming home to dead silence from my mom. No greeting and no response to my questions, just a hard wall of nothing. I would stand in front of her but she would stare straight ahead as though I weren't there.

During these periods of silence, my mom literally wouldn't say a word to us unless my dad was around. When he was present, she would converse with us kids as though everything was normal, but she would immediately slip back into silent mode when he left the room, went to bed, or left the house. We did not dare tell him she was doing this, or we would experience even prolonged punishment from her.

When you were in her good graces, she expected you to also give the silent treatment to the child who was on the "outs." She loved to talk badly about who was on the "outs" to anyone who would listen. My sister and I would share what she said with each other, but we had to do it very privately. If my mom found out we were talking to each other, the one on the "in" would quickly get moved to being on the "outs." And, inexplicably enough, the one who had been on the "outs" was now in the privileged spot of being her confidante. If there were two on the "outs," it wasn't so bad because you could commiserate with each other, but the worst was when you were the only one on the "outs." It was super lonely at home when you were the one who was completely ignored.

This emotional abuse was the cruelest for me, far outweighing any physical pain my dad could ever inflict on me. My dad's anger was always on the surface. When you made him angry, you usually could see what triggered him when he flew into a rage. You were able to anticipate when he might react negatively. With my mom, most of the time I had no clue as to what I did to cause her reactions.

She wouldn't take care of our basic needs when she was ignoring us, and we learned early to fend for ourselves. One time, when I was about ten years old, I became very ill at school and needed to go home. Feverish and sick to my stomach, I told the principal I also had swollen glands. Now, I really didn't know what swollen glands even were, but I had heard my sister saying she had them the last time she was sick.

The principal called my mom to come get me because it was cold and rainy out. My mom didn't want to leave the house, so I was told by the principal that my mom said I would have to walk home by myself. I didn't have an umbrella, so I arrived home a wet and feverish mess.

My mom was furious when she greeted me at the door. How dare I tell the principal I had swollen glands! He would think she was abusing me; how dare I put her in that position. She berated me while I stood in the living room dripping water on the floor. Feverish and shivering, all I wanted to do was to lie down under warm blankets and go to sleep. I begged her to let me go lay down, but she didn't respond. After a while, ignoring her demands to stay put, I peeled off my wet jacket and headed to my bedroom. I tried to block out her words while I took off my soaked clothes, pulled on my pajamas, and climbed into bed. She was still yelling at me when I drifted off to sleep.

I woke up to find myself on my mom's bad side, the recipient of her full silent treatment. I asked her for medicine to help me feel better. She ignored me, staring at the TV as though I wasn't even there. I asked her for something to drink. She sat in stone-cold silence. After a couple of minutes of trying to get her attention, I went back to bed and cried myself to sleep.

Pretending to be the doting mom, she finally brought me some medicine when my dad got home from work later that day. The silent treatment continued the whole time I was home sick, with Cheryl, who was thirteen at the time, taking care of me when she got home from school. She often had no choice but to step in and help when circumstances required it.

When I was in my mom's good graces, I felt accepted and she attended to my needs as best as she could. When she wasn't talking about other people, it felt good to be with her. She loved to converse about a variety of topics, and I reveled in the stories of her childhood. I was fascinated with her tales of growing up during World War II and picturing in my mind how our small town looked when she was a child. She always had the Cubs game on the TV, and I loved watching the games with her.

Our whole family would go to the mall every Friday night, having dinner at either McDonald's or a local diner. I was so excited when I became old enough to walk around the mall alone. I would spend what felt like hours looking at all the toys, especially the Barbie dolls, hoping I could convince my parents to buy me a small toy. On Saturday mornings we would do our weekly grocery shopping. My sister and I each got to pick out one small snack and one bottle of soda that would be our treats for the week.

In the warm weather, the whole family would pile in the car and drive to a local state park where we would spend the day picnicking and hiking on the trails. These were our family traditions, and this is when I most loved spending time with my mom.

When it came to us three kids, my mom favored my brother Bill. They spent a lot of time together, watching TV, smoking cigarettes, and drinking soda. Bill's dad had abandoned them when Bill was very young, and my mom raised him alone until she met my dad. She and Bill shared a special bond, and I believe she tried to make up for my father beating and bullying him most of the time.

My sister, while only three years older than I, had a maturity about her that made her my mom's confidante when my sister was in my mom's good graces. I was always jealous of their relationship. Cheryl became pregnant when she was fifteen, and while my parents freaked out about it at first, I think it made her a more suitable, mature companion for our mom. They would often go out shopping and for a bite to eat together. I would ask to join them but was always told I was too young to come along. I felt so left out and alone when they headed out, leaving me to stay home by myself.

If my dad was home and sober, I would hang out with him, either watching TV or sitting with him while he tinkered with his car. It began to feel like there was an "us" – me and my dad – and a "them" – my mom and my sister. I was happy I had him to spend time with, but that would be short-lived. To my utter shock and disbelief, my dad committed suicide when I was only twelve years old.

16

MY DAD'S SUICIDE

♥

The day began like any other Tuesday, except I wasn't feeling well when I woke up. I crawled out of bed and went downstairs to ask my mom if I could stay home from school. She agreed after taking one look at my pale face. When I started to go back upstairs to my bedroom, the phone rang. It was my grandma, looking for my dad. He hadn't shown up for work that morning at the family business.

My dad was an early riser, always out of the house before any of us would wake up. That morning, his car was still in the driveway, so my mom told my grandma that she assumed he rode his bicycle to work. The recent weather had been very mild, and he sometimes rode his bicycle to work instead of driving. My mom hung up the phone with my grandma, each promising to alert the other the minute they heard from my dad.

The early phone call woke up Bill and Cheryl, who had come downstairs to see what was going on. We discussed several theories about where our dad might be, our concern and doubt growing with each passing minute.

MY DAD'S SUICIDE

The day was cold and overcast with a chance of rain, not bike-riding weather.

There was little I could do so I went back upstairs to my bedroom to lie down. Minutes later, a loud noise erupted from the garage. It was the sound of a generator running amok. Startled, I ran downstairs to see what was going on. My dad kept his second car, an old red Ford Maverick, in the garage. Occasionally before heading off to work in the morning, he would start the car to see if the engine still ran. The garage door was closed but we knew there must be something wrong with the car. There was nothing else in the garage that could make this kind of noise.

My mom didn't know what to do, so she called the city to ask if someone could investigate. I'm sure she had an inkling of what might be discovered but kept it to herself. The city workers promptly arrived and went into our garage. The next thing I knew, one of them was at the door telling us they found my dad in the garage, sitting in the driver's side of the Maverick with all the car windows rolled up. The car was running and the noise we heard was the engine kicking into a high idle.

Cheryl and I stayed in the house, watching the events unfold while clinging to each other in tears and shock. We saw the men carry our dad out of the garage and place him on the concrete driveway. He was breathing but unconscious. The paramedics arrived and they kneeled on the ground next to him, trying to revive him.

I cried out when I saw them rip his favorite jacket from his body. My grandma had given my dad the blue windbreaker for his 52nd birthday only two months prior, and he wore it every day. I watched in horror as they lifted my dad onto the gurney and placed him in the ambulance to go to the hospital. That was the last time I ever saw my dad.

I felt helpless and thoughts were wildly running though my head. *This can't be happening to us. Daddy, why did you do this? I can't believe I am going to be one of "those" kids. Please, please, please don't die.* One thought stood out more than the others: *Please don't leave me alone with her!* "Her" was my mom.

I wasn't allowed to go to the hospital with my mom and sister. My mom said I was too young, and I was not feeling well. Later we realized the likely reason I was sick was due to the carbon monoxide fumes pouring from the Maverick, since my bedroom was right above the garage.

I lay on the couch all day trying to distract myself with the daytime TV shows, waiting to hear the news that my dad woke up. I kept thinking about the night before when he asked me to take a ride to Kmart with him. He seemed like he really wanted the company, but it was a beautiful spring evening and I wanted to hang out with one of my new friends. "Next time, I promise," I told him as I rode off on my bike, leaving him standing alone in the driveway.

Next time would never come, because my dad did not regain consciousness. At the hospital, the doctors told my mom his brain lost too much oxygen and the best prognosis was that he would remain in a comatose state for the remainder of his life. Sensing there was nothing more they could do that day, my mom and Cheryl came home in the early evening while he remained on life support in the ICU.

I didn't want to be alone, so my mom said I could sleep on the living room floor. My parents had never slept together as far back as I could remember. My dad slept in their bedroom and my mom slept on the living room couch every night. Even though he wasn't there, I didn't want to be in his bed, preferring to arrange my blankets and pillow on the living room floor next to the couch. My brother stayed with us, falling asleep in one of the living room chairs. Cheryl retired to her bedroom upstairs.

I had drifted off to sleep when the phone rang, just after 10 p.m. It was the hospital informing my mom that my dad had just passed away. She hung up the phone and came back into the living room, bent down over me, and said "Amy, that was the hospital. Your daddy just died." This was the most compassion I ever felt from my mom in my whole life, and the first time she ever referred to my dad as "daddy." She then went upstairs to give my sister the news. As my mom left the room, my brother exclaimed, "Thank god that bastard is gone."

I woke up the next morning to a whole new world. The day felt like a cruel mockery of what had just happened to me. Unlike the gray and overcast day before, it was a beautiful spring day, warm and sunny. Outside, people were going about their normal lives. To me, it was surreal. How could everyone go about like nothing happened? My dad had just committed suicide. And my life would never be the same.

I had no outlet for my grief. My mom showed little compassion toward me and did not provide any guidance for how to cope with the loss of my father. I was discouraged from showing any emotion or even talking about his death. I tried to talk to some of my friends, but they could not relate. I felt completely alone.

A few days after my dad passed away, my mom and I walked to a local diner to have lunch before going to pick up a few groceries from the market. To say the meal was awkward is an understatement. My mom and I rarely spent time alone together. Sitting across from her in the booth, I didn't know what to say or how to act. I wanted to find some common ground and let my mom know I was trying my best to cope with my dad's death but, at twelve, it was hard to bring my thoughts into words. I also wanted to get reassurance from her that everything was going to be okay in the long run. That we as a family were going to be okay.

"Maybe after going through Dad's death, I will be able to deal with your death better when you die", I said to my mom, trying to start a conversation around the difficulty I was having in coping with his death. Maybe it was an odd thing to say to her, but I didn't know how to talk to my mom about everyday topics, much less convey my grief to her. Part of me wanted to reassure my mom that I could be a mature person who would not be a burden to her. But I was in pain, looking for the compassion and support that I desperately needed to feel from her. Coming from this place of deep need and vulnerability, I was not prepared for the viciousness of her response.

"So, you want me to die?", my mom hissed at me. Taken aback, I tried to explain what I meant, that no I didn't want her to die. I told her I didn't know how to deal with my dad's death, but I would learn from it, and she wouldn't have to worry about me in the future, after she was gone. She ignored my response, telling me to finish up so we could leave the restaurant. I lost my appetite but forced myself to eat what was on my plate. A heavy silence fell over us while she got a doggy bag for her leftover food and paid the bill.

As we walked to the grocery store, my mom began attacking me for what I said. Over and over, she ranted about how I wished she was dead and how she couldn't believe I would be more upset about my dad dying than her death. Maybe I would even celebrate her death. She knew that I didn't care about her at all and maybe she should have died instead of him. She would not let me defend myself, instead talking over my pleas while I continued to try to explain what I meant.

I was in tears by the time we got to the grocery store. Before we went in, she ordered me to dry up my crocodile tears. She said she knew I wasn't really upset because it would make me happy to see her dead. I went off on my own in the store to compose myself.

When I met up with her at the deli counter, she greeted me like nothing was wrong. Putting on a show in front of the deli worker, she acted as though she was happy to see me. She continued to be pleasant while we went through the checkout line, but the minute we walked out the front door, her entire demeanor switched to one of anger.

She ignored me the entire walk home, even when I tried to talk to her, and she didn't speak to me for the rest of the day. I never again brought up the impact of my father's death on me, and she also chose to ignore the topic. However, she never let me forget what transpired that day.

A couple of weeks after my dad died, my best friend's family invited me on their summer vacation, a driving trip from Illinois to Washington state and back. Oh, how bad I wanted to go, to get away from my family and experience the western United States! My mom said no at first. She didn't want me to leave so soon after my dad died. In an odd way, it made me feel good to know she had concerns about me and my whereabouts. But I really wanted to go, I needed to get away. Thanks to my near-constant begging and my friend's mom's reassurances of my well-being, my mom relented. I loved that trip, seeing our beautiful country firsthand, and being a kid with my needs taken care of by my friend's parents. For those two weeks, I forgot about my situation at home. It was the first time in my life I was able to escape the drama of my family, and I relished that freedom from fear.

17

A WHOLE NEW WORLD

———— ♥ ————

After my dad died, we tried to fall back into some sense of normalcy but nothing ever quite jelled for us. We had few family rituals left before his death and my mom wasn't interested in starting any new ones. Our lack of togetherness as a family was partly due to us kids getting older and wanting to hang out with friends on the weekends, but my parents also seemed to grow disinterested in being with each other.

We hadn't eaten dinner together as a family since I was a small child. When my dad was alive, dinner was served like clockwork at 4:30 every afternoon when he got home from work. He would get to fill up his plate first and then retire to the living room to watch TV while eating dinner. It didn't matter where we ate or if we were even home for dinner. There was barely enough food to go around, so if you wanted to eat, you made sure to be home on time.

After my dad died, my mom stopped cooking on most days. There was no need to have dinner ready at any particular time, so we were basically left to fend for ourselves. If we were lucky, there might be a TV dinner, a box of macaroni and cheese, or fixings for a grilled cheese or tuna sandwich in the house.

My mom didn't know how to drive, always relying on my dad or others to take her where she needed to go. Because she had cut off relationships with most of her family and friends, we took to walking to and from the grocery store, our arms barely able to carry the heavy bags during the mile walk. I remember having to stop and rest often while I tried to keep the bags from spilling from my skinny arms.

After my dad's death, my mom struggled with looking for work. She had no marketable skills and made only a couple half-hearted attempts to apply for jobs. I'll never know how she thought she would be able to support us over the long haul. There was a small insurance payout from my dad's death but instead of saving it, my mom went on a spending spree, buying new appliances and clothes. What little remained would not last long.

The bulk of our household income came from the Social Security checks Cheryl and I were entitled to after our dad died. My mom received $350 a month for each of us. While $700 a month surely didn't seem like a lot of money, it would soon drop to $350 when my sister moved out at age sixteen after giving birth to her son, Christopher.

This left me at home with my mom and Bill, who by then was an adult in his twenties. All three of us lived on the $350 per month Social Security check which was supplemented sporadically with government food stamps. While we were poor when my dad was alive, we were now sinking into depths of poverty I could not have imagined.

My parents purchased a house less than a year before my dad took his life. It was more than 100 years old, very creepy, and fell in the fixer-upper category. Shortly after we moved in, major plumbing issues surfaced that drained much of my parent's budget. After my dad died, when something broke, it just didn't get fixed. There was no money to hire outside contractors and my mom was not handy around the house. First, the dryer stopped working, then the washing machine. The upstairs bathroom was soon out of commission when the plumbing backed up and the floor began to leak into the downstairs hallway.

Rats invaded the house, first chewing their way through every box that was in the attic. The loud, steady hum of their gnawing teeth was an eerie sound that echoed through our house in the dead of night. We could have salvaged some of our belongings, but I was too afraid to go into the attic alone and my mom ignored the problem.

Soon the rats became braver and started making appearances in the kitchen during the day, looking for food when they thought no one was in there. I lived in fear of walking around the house at night. I would lean into a room to turn the light on, poised to run in the opposite direction if I saw a rat. More than once I was greeted by a big rat sitting on the kitchen counter, staring me down with its beady little eyes until I ran screaming from the room.

My mom was frozen when it came to taking care of the maintenance of the house or exterminating the rats. She could not consistently pay the mortgage and we lived each month with the reality of foreclosure one step away. I had many sleepless nights, worrying about being homeless.

At sixteen, I knew the only solution was to give up the house. I found a small apartment in the newspaper that sounded like a perfect place for my mom and me to live. I set up an appointment to see it and talked to the owner about our situation. She agreed to rent to us, and I created a budget that covered how we could afford it as well as our other bills. I brought the proposal to my mom, but she flat out refused to consider it. My plan didn't include my brother, who was twenty-nine and unemployed. She didn't want to live without him.

My personal needs were rarely met. In my freshman year of high school, I owned one pair of jeans, two pairs of shoes, and a few tops. Luckily, I had some generous and caring friends who would loan me clothes from time to time. My mom somehow managed to always have money for cigarettes and soda for herself and my brother but she rarely would give me money for basic personal hygiene items like shampoo, feminine care, soap, and toothpaste. I had no choice but to become creative to get what I most needed.

When I was fourteen, I started doing most of our grocery shopping by myself. If I didn't, I would have no food to eat. I walked to and from the market, lugging heavy grocery bags. It didn't matter if the weather was hot, cold, snowy, rainy, or sunny. Unless I was in her good graces, I would have to beg my mom to give me food stamps. Whether or not she complied depended on her mood. If she said no, there was little food for me at home. I would often go to a friend's house, hoping they would offer me something to eat. Otherwise, I would have to wait for my mom's mood to change until I could get food. Thanks to my high metabolism, I felt like I was in a near-constant state of hunger for much of my teen years.

To buy personal hygiene items, I became creative in how I shopped for food. Food stamps were valid only for food items and not for products like soap, shampoo, and conditioner. When you paid with food stamps, your change consisted of food stamps in dollar increments and coins when under a dollar. To get enough coins to buy personal items, I would make multiple trips through the checkout lane to get as close to 99 cents change back each time. I would repeat this process until I had enough money to buy the items I desperately needed.

After our washer and dryer stopped working when I was fourteen, it became my responsibility to take our laundry to the laundromat. Sometimes, my mom gave me extra money for a taxi, or a friend would drive me. Other times I would walk, carrying laundry detergent and a large heavy bag of clothes and linens over a mile to and from the laundromat. My mom gave me exact change for the number of loads I was doing and not a penny more. When she was giving me the silent treatment, she would not give me any money to do laundry so I would wash my clothes in the kitchen sink and hang them to dry. Sometimes, if I was lucky, I could wash my clothes at a friend's house if their parents allowed it.

My mom was not able to afford health insurance, so I was only allowed to go to the doctor or dentist for real emergencies. Preventive care was a luxury we could not afford.

When I was sixteen, I developed two cavities in my bottom molars that were a source of constant, excruciating pain. My mom forbade me to go to the dentist, so I began consuming large doses of aspirin to cope with the throbbing. I would wake up crying in the middle of the night when the effects of the aspirin had worn off. My mom wouldn't buy the aspirin for me, so I'd use the change from the food stamps to buy as many bottles as I could, forgoing other items I desperately needed.

The constant pain became unbearable and I was desperate for relief. After living in agony for over a month, I defied my mom's orders and went to a dentist on my own. I'm sure he knew he would not get reimbursed for his work, but taking pity on my situation, he filled the cavities for me. My mom was livid when she discovered what I had done but I honestly didn't care. It felt so good to be free of the constant pain.

As far back as I can remember, I lived with the endless perception of lack. It was a horrible feeling, empty yet all-consuming. I had a deep hunger to experience both the basics and the fullness of life. But abundance was a gift that was bestowed upon a chosen group of people that didn't include me. My friends would receive new clothes, go on vacations with their family, and have spending money on a regular basis. My experience was in such stark contrast, causing my self-esteem to suffer since I felt less deserving than others.

As a teenager, I wanted to earn my own money, but it was hard to find consistent work, since my hometown was in tough economic times. A factory that had been the main employer for the town moved its operation south in the '70s. It was still struggling in the '80s and jobs were few and far between, especially for a teenager with few skills.

One of our neighbors across the street ran an industrial laundry on their property. When I was thirteen, they hired me to work alongside Cheryl, and paid me $2 an hour in cash. The small facility was blistering hot and the work was hard. Drenched in sweat, we moved heavy, wet hospital sheets from washers to dryers and then folded them to be pressed. I worked a few days a week and I was beyond happy with having my own money to spend. I was crushed when, out of the blue, my mom made me quit, declaring the owners were violating child-labor laws.

During the summer of my sixteenth year, I applied to a work program for children from low-income families and I was accepted for a job at the local YMCA. It was really hard work, mostly manual labor. But it was fun, and I made friends with other kids who came from families that were struggling financially.

We were tasked with whatever the Y staff needed us to do. We cleaned the entire building; nothing was left untouched. We scrubbed the windows, racquetball courts, gym equipment, bathrooms, and locker rooms. We tended to the large grounds and we helped the office staff address flyers to be sent out to the members. My favorite days were when I was assigned to help with the day care. I loved watching over the toddlers, and I developed a close bond with some of the children.

The YMCA job was full-time, and I was paid the minimum wage of $3.35. While that's not a lot of money to most people, for the first time in my life I had serious cash. I was able to buy myself everything I lacked – clothes, food, makeup, and personal hygiene products. I had spending money to go places with my friends, outings that I had declined in the past. Unfortunately, this abundance was short-lived because the job ended when summer was over.

That summer, my mom's mental health began to severely decline. She had almost fully sequestered herself in our house, only occasionally venturing out for a quick errand. She had cut herself off from her family and friends. She stopped taking their calls and no longer visited with them. My brother ran most of her errands, picking up cigarettes or take-out food for the two of them.

My mom began playing favorites more and more. My brother was almost always on her good side, which meant I was either being given the silent treatment or on the receiving end of a barrage of criticism. She criticized my looks, my friends, my weight, the way I talked, the way

I walked, the music I listened to, and so on. She told me I looked like my father, and that it was my fault he died. She said I was crazy, and no one liked me. She told me I was pretty on the outside but ugly on the inside. She told me she was surprised I wasn't retarded or born with other birth defects, since she was an older mom when she had me. She said I was an accident, a child she never wanted, and she wished she had gotten an illegal abortion instead of having me.

I would yell back at her out of frustration and pain; the only defense I had was trying to use words to hurt her the way she was hurting me. Maybe then it would stop. It never did. She was Teflon, nothing stuck. I would escape to my room, her words following me upstairs. I would turn my rock music on as loud as I could to drown out her voice while she continued to deliver the criticisms of me. Many times, after being upstairs for an hour or so, I would shut off my music to hear her still talking to herself, ranting as though I were still within earshot.

It was around this time my anxiety began to show in my outward appearance. This is when I first experienced hyperhidrosis, the extreme sweating under my arms, and the shaking of my hands. I started hanging out with older kids in sophomore year, and we would drink alcohol whenever we hung out. It provided a means to escape the pain I did not know how to deal with.

I had no relationships with any of my relatives and felt completely alone. Cheryl was now living far from home and I always looked to her for guidance whenever we had a chance to talk on the phone. Back then, it cost a lot of money to call long distance, so I had to wait for her to call me.

The only refuge from my mom was leaving the house, which I did every chance I got. At fifteen, I began staying out all night or sleeping at a friend's house whenever I could, anything that would keep me away from my situation at home.

18

FINAL DAYS

As my mom's mental health deteriorated, her behavior toward me became even more erratic. She started hiding dishes in her bedroom so I couldn't use them. On more than one occasion, when I was cooking or eating, she snatched up the dishes I was using. After washing them, she hid them in her dresser, telling me that they belonged to her and I was not allowed to use them.

Another time, my mom started a fight with me and my friend, Mary, while we were in the kitchen. While swearing at Mary and calling her bad names, my mom snatched up the dishes we were using and brought them to her bedroom. Coming back into the kitchen, she ordered me to leave the house and not come back. When I wouldn't go, she hit me over the head with a heavy wooden dustpan brush. The blow was so hard I needed to go the hospital. It was the first time she ever hit me.

The hospital contacted the authorities and soon I started to see Julie, the school therapist, on a regular basis. Julie was a blessing for me, the first adult in my life who I felt was on my side. She spent some time with my mom before we started our sessions. My mom told Julie stories of how terrible I was and painted herself as the victim. Julie saw through it, recognizing that my mom was struggling with mental and emotional issues. I relished every minute I spent with Julie, as they were the only moments of sanity I had with any adult in my life.

Not long after we started meeting, Julie felt that her training as a school therapist wasn't the right fit for the help I needed so she referred me to Mark, a psychologist trained in family counseling. Mark agreed to take me as a pro-bono client, and he was truly a lifesaver for me. He was my salvation and I eagerly looked forward to our weekly sessions. I could talk to him about everything going on in my life and he always made me see how worthy I was beyond the situation I was having to deal with at home.

Shortly after I turned seventeen, my mom laid down on the couch and basically didn't get up again. She would lie there all day and all night, the TV constantly on. She started talking about wanting to die. She was on a mission to die. She said she was going to stop taking her blood pressure medicine because she knew it was the only thing keeping her alive. She said she knew I wanted her to die and she knew that nobody cared about her. She would tell Cheryl all this when Cheryl called to check in. My mom completely gave up on her life and she wanted us to feel guilty about it.

I begged Mark to help me get help for her but there was nothing he could do. By law, you could not force someone to go to counseling without their permission. While I was constantly hurting from the emotional pain she inflicted on me, she was my mom and I didn't want her to die. I wanted her to be healthy and I often daydreamed about having a normal mother-daughter relationship with her. Unfortunately, there was nothing I could do to help her.

From the couch, she still played her games of manipulation, pitting my brother and me against each other. Rarely was I on her good side; she was either giving me the silent treatment or pummeling me with endless verbal abuse.

One day when my mom and I were fighting, she pulled my brother into it. Bill hit me and pushed me to the floor. When he was trying to hit me again, she yelled, "I hope you kill her!" sitting up excitedly from her place on the couch. I was scared to death. I could take all the verbal and emotional abuse but, for the first time in my life, I was frightened that I could die at the hands of my own family. What hurt even more is that I truly believed that in her declined mental state, my mom was saying what she really felt.

I turned to Cheryl, who was now living in the suburbs of Chicago, the mom of two small children and going through a divorce. I called her from the kitchen, whispering so my mom wouldn't hear as I told Cheryl what happened. She instructed me to leave immediately and go to my friend Mary's house. I quickly threw a bag together, a small one so as not to arouse suspicion, and without saying a word to my mom, I escaped the house. Within hours, my sister and her friend arrived at Mary's to bring me back to my sister's home in the suburbs. Two hours later, when we arrived at my sister's home, I felt a sense of safety and relief that I hadn't known in years – mixed in with dread that I would have to go back home at some point.

I called Mark the next day to tell him what happened. He instructed me not to contact my mom. He wanted to give her the chance to file a missing person's report. If she didn't file one within three days, it would be considered child neglect and then my sister could petition to be the recipient of my Social Security benefit on my behalf. Before we ended the call, he told me he was relieved I had run away. He said that since our first session, he wanted to tell me to do just that, but it was obviously not something he could legally advise me to do, given I was a minor. Mark said that during every session he wished he could take a magic wand and go poof! and I would magically be whisked away from my home situation.

I wasn't sure what to expect. I had taken to coming and going as I pleased from our house, but I was never gone for more than a night and, when she was talking to me, I would tell my mom where I was going to be. At the end of three days, she hadn't reported me as missing and we were now at the point where we could petition Social Security, a decision not easy for either me or Cheryl.

The choice was really between who would be financially cared for, me or my mom. We knew taking the money from her was going to put her in a position to have no income whatsoever, and she had no skills to find a job. Yet she spent little of the money on my care. She felt I was a burden and the only value I brought to her was the money. If I didn't claim the Social Security, I would have nowhere to live. Cheryl was in no financial position to support me on her own. We had no other family members to whom we could go for help. None of them seemed to want to have a relationship with us, much less open their homes and wallets for me.

With heavy hearts, Cheryl and I moved forward with making the Social Security petition. We returned to my hometown to file the documents and meet with the case worker. Mark attended the meeting, bearing witness to my mom's neglect of me. Afterward, my friend Mary drove me to my mom's house so I could get some of my belongings. We felt it was best for Cheryl not to come with me given the situation with Social Security. I was scared to death when Mary dropped me off. Instead of waiting in front of the house, we decided she would park around the corner and come back for me in fifteen minutes.

When I walked in the front door of the house, my mom was laying in her usual position on the living room couch. She gave me a dirty look but didn't greet me or try to stop me from coming in. Nor did she ask me where I had been or what I had been doing in the days I had been gone. I ran to my room and quickly gathered up as much as I could carry. I was waiting for Mary on the porch with my small pile of belongings, when my mom came out and snatched up one of my pillows, telling me it was hers and I couldn't have it. When I said ok, she stormed back into the house, slamming the door behind her. Unbeknownst to me at the time, this was the last exchange of words I would ever have with my mom.

Back in the suburbs, Cheryl and I tried to live as much of a normal life as possible while we waited to hear the decision from the Social Security Administration. Cheryl's children, Christopher and Sarah, were a much-welcome distraction from the stress. We would sometimes go to Cheryl's friend Marcie's house, where Marcie and her mom tried their best to make me feel welcome. They were concerned with how thin I was and tried to feed me every time I visited. I had no appetite and would barely pick at the plates piled high with food they put in front of me.

Marcie and her mom were a jovial pair, but it was hard for me to open up to them while I was processing the trauma I had experienced. I felt awkward and out of place.

Out of concern for my well-being, they often commented that I looked like I was on the verge of a nervous breakdown with my shaking hands and tense face. It was true, I definitely felt like I was barely holding myself together.

Soon after visiting their offices, the Social Security administration granted our petition, and Cheryl would now receive the monthly check on my behalf. We celebrated my freedom while in the back of our minds we feared what might happen to my mom. The outcome came sooner than we expected.

A couple of weeks after the petition was granted, my mom was rushed to the hospital after collapsing from a heart attack. Cheryl and I were not able to see her immediately, given we were two hours away and neither of us had driver's licenses. My sister talked to the doctor over the phone who explained that our mom had stopped taking her blood-pressure medicine. The doctor told us she had warned her repeatedly not to stop, that she would certainly die if her blood pressure was not kept under control.

A few days later, one of our friends drove us to our hometown to see our mom. She was still in the hospital and was conscious, so we were allowed to see her. She glared at us when we entered the room. I was so afraid of my mom that I could barely say a word. I couldn't take the look of hate and anger I saw coming from her eyes. After only a few minutes, I ran out of the room crying. I did not know how to deal with the heaviness and the dark emotions of the situation.

Moments later, with Cheryl at her bedside, our mom experienced another heart attack and quickly passed away. Cheryl came out to tell me the news and said that right before our mom died, she mouthed the words, "You put me here." And just like that, we were both motherless and I was an orphan at age seventeen.

After my mom's death, we found a suicide note in her wallet, dated shortly before her first heart attack. The letter was not addressed to anyone in particular. In it, my mom wrote about how she never felt loved her whole life, that her children did not treat her well, and that she didn't want to live any longer.

For decades, I lived with deep guilt for taking the Social Security money from my mom. While it was inevitable she would not be able to rely on my Social Security payments once I turned eighteen, neither Cheryl nor I felt good about the abrupt ending of her life. I felt my mom would not have stopped taking her medications if she didn't have to worry about the money. Her last words to Cheryl also added to deep feelings of uncertainty about whether we did the right thing by taking my Social Security payments from her.

Healing that guilt took some time, given how deep it ran in me. I've learned guilt can help you to expand your consciousness by showing you where you are out of alignment with your True Self, but you need to heal it to move forward. If you are feeling guilty about anything, I recommend you transform that feeling to love as soon as possible. Guilt carries a low vibration, and, regardless of what's happened, it is not beneficial to anyone to feel this way.

If you are experiencing guilt, you can overcome it. Healing guilt requires that you first forgive yourself for the act. Releasing the dense, negative energy of guilt from your body using The Release Technique in this book will also speed up the healing. It's important to go easy on yourself. Remember, we are all always doing our best given our current level of consciousness.

19

ON BEING A PARENT

After my traumatic childhood, I was hesitant to become a parent myself. Would I create an environment that was scary and unwelcoming to a child? Was I worthy of being a parent? Would I be able to give my children the love all children need? While I had a lot of hands-on practice with kids from taking care of my niece and nephew, I wouldn't know what kind of parent I would be until I became one myself.

I was also terrified of physically having children, so much so that I remember telling my friends as early as five years old that I was only going to adopt. My mom always talked about how hard pregnancy was on her, and how giving birth to me almost killed her. My birth was a Cesarean section, and, after four other kids, it was hard on my mom's frail body. One of my brothers who was born two years before me was also a Cesarean section, and he only lived several hours after birth. He was born prematurely due to my dad's abuse of my mom.

After having both of my daughters, I feel to this day that becoming a mom is the best thing I have ever done in my life. All the deep fears of childbirth proved to be unfounded. For all my worries, I had very easy experiences with both of my daughter's births.

It was my decision to split up with my ex-husband two years after awakening to my True Self, when our daughters were 5 and 3. Ending a marriage is not an easy thing, especially when children are involved, but I was at a point in my life where I needed to be true to my need to heal and grow, and to make choices in my life that are driven by moving toward what I want instead of moving away in fear. As I said at the start of this book, my ex-husband is a good guy, and we made the decision to always put our two girls' best interests first. We share custody of them, and I am grateful that he and I have a very strong co-parenting partnership to this day.

Since I have my girls only 50% of the time, I consider myself a part-time single mom. Being a parent is hard enough, but being a solo parent brings along its own unique set of challenges, especially with maintaining consistency for my daughters across two households. This is where I can count on their dad to create a similar experience for the girls no matter which house they are at.

Being a parent is both one of the most joyful and one of the most difficult roles I have ever taken on. I have been entrusted with the care of these two beautiful beings, to guide them in life, see they are healthy, and have their basic needs met. I want to shield them from all hurt and harm that may come their way. When they hurt, I feel it in my body. When they are happy, it lights up my soul.

The toughest thing I face is learning to let go of them. Not just when they go off to college but as they experience everyday life lessons today. I can support their basic needs and give them direction, but I can't live their lives for them.

They, too, are infinite beings who are here for their own soul growth and they need to experience all the good and bad that comes their way. They need to do the work to discover their True Selves and they will, when the time is right. I cannot do this for them, but I can show them the way when they are ready. They will decide if and when to step on the path, and they will take the leap when the time is right for their soul's evolution.

20

LIGHT OF DIVINITY WITHIN

♥

You may be wondering what has kept me going through all the adversity to create the life I have today. One where I am financially stable, have two beautiful daughters, a successful career, friends I cherish, and relationships with my family that are so filled with love. I am no longer wracked by stress and anxiety all day. I walk around in a state of peace more often than not. When distress appears within, I know how to handle it. I still have a long way to go on my soul's journey, but I have the support and tools now to proactively deal with what appears in my life, situation by situation. I am now consciously creating my life the way I want it to be from the place of my True Self.

During my life, through all the trials and trauma, all the guilt and shame I experienced, I always felt a light, centered in my heart space, that burned bright and steady within me. Somehow, I knew no matter what I did or said, all would ultimately be okay. I felt it. This light kept me going and no matter how difficult things became, this light would eventually propel me to move forward in a positive way.

Today, I know the light to be the energy of God. I am a unique emanation of God. I know this from the light that is always present within me. It's become my quest to bring more of this power through me and to be able to share with others how to do the same.

By understanding my True Self, I have the power to create my world. Try it yourself. Get familiar with that light within you. Learn it, feel it, and encourage it to grow. Do not let anyone or anything take you away from this power. Spend every minute of every hour of every day doing what you can to uncover more of it. It's not easy, but you can do it. By following the techniques I share with you in this book, you will accelerate the realization of this power. When you practice these exercises regularly, it's inevitable that you will soon be living your life from your True Self.

The light was always within me, even when I didn't realize it. I always looked to improve myself, to be on par with the light. It's a voice within that nudges me to look at myself regularly, what I am doing, and where I am in life. It prompts me to ask myself, "If I do nothing differently, this is the best I will ever be in my life. Is that okay?" I do this with every facet of my life. Sometimes it's okay and sometimes it's not. When it's not, I now use all the tools I share in this book to create something different, aligned with what I really want.

21

TRUE-SELF EXERCISES

♥

Method: Affirmations

A powerful way to consciously attract what you want is by using affirmations. Affirmations are positive statements that often start with "I AM" followed by that which you want to create in this world. Affirmations are the powerful words of creation; "I AM" is your imagination. The power goes beyond that of positive thinking. When your life energy and beliefs are aligned to your "I AM" statements, you can expect your desires to appear in your life experience.

How many times have you heard someone say, "I am going to catch that cold" and sure enough, they catch the cold? Or start complaining "I am getting old" and before you know it, they have aged ten years in six months? "I AM" statements are a direct request to God for what you want. Wouldn't it be better to put what you want after those words instead of what you don't want?

I cannot stress strongly enough that your beliefs and feelings must be aligned to an affirmation for it to manifest in your physical experience. If you affirm, "I am young," but really believe and feel "I am old," then you will not attract youth into your experience. You will attract aging. Your alignment in body and mind to an affirmation is a great predictor of what is going to show up in your experience. It's important to use the feelings in your body to gauge your affiliation to an affirmation. The mind focuses on its conscious thoughts and cannot access the depths of your subconscious the way your body can. This makes your body a powerful co-creator of your experience.

Ultimately, you must align your life energy to that which you want to create in the affirmation. You can test how you feel about an "I AM" statement by using the Release Technique. After you have connected to your heart space, repeat the "I AM" statement and see what comes up for you in your thoughts and in your body. Keep releasing until you have shifted the energy so that you are in harmony with the intention of the affirmation.

It's not uncommon to state an affirmation and have the exact opposite materialize in your life. When this happens, most people quickly declare that this is evidence that affirmations do not work and immediately stop using them. The reality is that the affirmation is working exactly as it should. It is showing you where you have limiting beliefs that are out of alignment with your True Self, and what you need to heal before that which is affirmed can appear in your life. After all, life is a mirror that reflects your state of consciousness. When an affirmation shows you what you really believe, it is a good time to express gratitude for it easily showing you these buried limiting beliefs.

How to Practice Affirmations:

1. Compose your affirmation. Say what it is you want, not what you don't want. Use the present tense, as though you already have what it is that you want. For example:

If you want…	Affirm this:	Not this:
Health	I AM healthy	I am not sick
Wealth	I AM wealthy	I am not poor
Success	I AM successful	I am not going to fail
Significant other	I AM in a loving relationship	I am not alone

2. Begin with the "Connect to Your Heart Space" exercise.
3. Say your affirmation aloud.
4. Check in with your body and mind when you say the statement. "Fake it 'til you make it" doesn't work with affirmations. Your feelings and beliefs must be aligned to the outcome you want to experience.
5. Use the Release Technique to clear any resistance you may feel.
6. Repeat the above three steps until you feel no resistance in your body and mind.
7. To super-charge the power of your "I AM" statement to manifest what you desire, add the visualization process I share in the next section.

TRUE-SELF EXERCISES

Below are examples of affirmations I have used that can also help you in your expansion into your True Self.

- I AM love.
- I AM worthy of giving and receiving love.
- I AM connected to all others. We are one.
- I AM whole, perfect, strong, powerful, loving, harmonious, and happy. (from *The Master Key* by Charles Haanel)
- I AM perfect just the way I am.
- I AM always surrounded by love.
- I AM moving forward easily and effortlessly in all aspects of my life.
- I AM exactly where I am supposed to be, right here and right now.
- I AM allowing life to unfold easily and effortlessly.
- I AM open to receiving new ideas on my next steps and I take inspired action to get there.
- I AM a masterful creator of my life experience and today I choose to deliberately create what I desire.
- I AM willing to release the idea of who and what I have been to receive the new.
- I AM a powerful creator with limitless potential.
- I AM love and I experience abundance in all aspects of my life.
- I AM able to bounce back from all adversity with ease and grace.
- I AM worthy of attracting loving and committed people into my life.
- I AM fully supported as I embark on my adventure of transformation.

- I AM perfect health in every cell of my being.
- I AM fully embracing my True Self starting now.

Affirmations are truly the gift of creation. They are the creative words from God. Combined with visualization, they will make you unstoppable in whatever you wish to achieve.

Method: Visualization

Visualizing is the practice of using your imagination to create what you want to experience in your life. It can be done in a few simple steps. There is no reason to complicate it and you should have fun with it. You can get as big as you want with what you are asking; just make sure your beliefs and feelings are aligned with the result you are seeking.

Visualization is a very important tool in creating your desired outcome. We use our imagination to define what we want and solidify it by also engaging in the feeling of our desire once it manifests. Feeling is very important, since it creates the vibration that attracts our wish to us and accelerates how quickly it comes to us. If you have trouble picturing in your mind what you want, you can focus on the feeling only and still get remarkable results.

While practicing visualization, it's important to add as many details as possible. Try to create a vision in which all your senses can engage. If you are visualizing a new car, picture sitting in the driver's seat while taking in the new-car smell. Look through the windshield and notice what you see. Are you on a busy street? Are people walking by and are they happy? Hear the other traffic around you.

Picture lifting your coffee cup from the cup-holder in the center console and notice how good this coffee tastes in your new car. Feel in your body the joy while you drive this new car on your favorite scenic route. Spare no detail and have fun with this. Remember, everything that exists in the world today is here through the use of imagination.

How to Practice Visualization:

1. Begin with the "Connect to Your Heart Space" exercise. Visualizing should be done in the most joyful and loving state you can be.
2. With your eyes closed, picture what you want as though you have it right now. It's that simple. Engage all five senses. Feel within your body how it feels to have that which you are visualizing.
3. Do this for at least five minutes every day and end the session when you can no longer align your feelings with the vision.
4. Have fun with it!
5. Feel gratitude for the outcome and go about your day.

Method: Intentions

You can consciously create your life by intending the experiences and interactions you wish to manifest while you go about the day. Do you want your spouse to show appreciation for you making dinner at night? Intend it! A productive meeting with a group of people who are usually adversarial? Intend it! Harmonious family dinner time? A glowing review about your recent performance on a big project along with a generous salary increase from your boss? Intention is the key.

How to Set Intentions:
1. Take a moment to pause each time you move from one situation to another throughout the day.
2. Begin with the "Connect to Your Heart Space" exercise.
3. Use an affirmation to set the intention for what you wish to experience.
4. Quickly visualize the outcome.
5. Create the feelings in your body of how you want to feel.
6. Feel gratitude for the outcome and go about your day.

What shows up in your experience will indicate if you are in alignment to the intention. Use the Release Technique the next time you set an intention if you feel resistance to it, or if the manifestation is not aligned to your desires.

At first, it may be difficult to remember to set intentions. We've lived our whole life to this point on autopilot and creating a new habit is never easy. Our days are fast-paced, and we move so quickly from one experience to another. To ease yourself into this, I suggest creating an alert on your phone for a few minutes before the hour of every waking hour. When alerted, pause what you are doing and set your intention for the events of the upcoming hour. You may not be able to stop every time but doing it only a few times a day will have an amazing impact on the events of your life. If you regularly practice the technique, you will develop the habit of creating your life as you move throughout your day.

Method: Receiving

Once you ask God for what you desire through affirmations, visualizations, and intentions, you need to be open to receiving what comes your way. You must believe it is going to come and that you are worthy of it. You need to allow it to come into your life.

How does one become open? Use the Release Technique and focus on openness in your body. You will notice where your body is open and where you feel tension. Where you feel tension or resistance is where you need to clear the energy to receive. Breathe into it, release it, let the feelings and associated thoughts go.

You need to be alert and look for clues to where God is bringing you what you asked for. What appears in your life may not be precisely what you were expecting or come to you exactly how you wanted it to, but you will find it is perfectly right for you. It may require you to act but it will always be inspired action, not forced. You will intuitively know the next step for you.

22

MY SHIFT TO INNER PEACE AND CALM

♥

When anxiety was my normal state, it was painful and exhausting to live with the steady buzz of negative energy in my body, day in and day out. I tried to numb myself with food, alcohol, and exercise, but the anxiety always played in the background of my life.

Developing inner peace required me to take on the work of healing the negativity in my being. I had a lot of baggage from this lifetime alone, not to mention whatever I was carrying in my DNA from my ancestors. This wasn't going to be easy. With open eyes, I set off on the path to healing, accelerating my transformation by consciously facing the suffering I experienced head-on.

Using the techniques I am teaching you in the book, as well as super-charging my growth by working with master life energy coaches, I was able to start living from my True Self, where I largely feel calm and at ease within my body and Ego Mind most of the time. I think far fewer thoughts of fear, judgment, lack, and separation. Don't get me wrong; this is a process of constant evolution. Situations continue to arise that pull me back into a state of anxiety and negative Ego Mind, especially given my sensitive nature. However, I am more conscious when this happens now, and I can readily use the tools I've learned to transform myself back to a state of inner peace.

As I shifted my energy to my True Self, I began to attract into my life that which I wanted to experience. My being was no longer bogged down with negative energy, but instead emanating the light from within.

23

LONELINESS

♥

Loneliness is one of the worst feelings anyone can experience. Loneliness occurs when you feel no one cares and you have no connection to others. Anxiety often accompanies loneliness, further accentuating the feeling of isolation. Much of our population experiences loneliness. Cigna Health's 2018 Loneliness Index found that 46 percent of Americans report feeling lonely sometimes or always, and 47 percent report feeling left out sometimes or always. Loneliness can lead to other adverse outcomes such as overeating, depression, substance abuse, illness, and in worst cases, suicide.

Loneliness has been a constant theme in my life, its roots running deep in my childhood. Whether I have been by myself, in a room with a handful of people, or in a crowd of thousands, I have felt the crushing sense of loneliness many times. Because of my life experience, I didn't always know how to relate to people, especially if they seemed to have a "normal" life. I felt out of place in many social situations, like an alien around "normal" people.

LONELINESS

When I was a child, I often felt lonely because I felt like no one cared about me. My parents were wrapped up in their own problems most of the time. My older siblings didn't have a lot in common with me, so they didn't spend a lot of time with me. Outside of my time spent with friends, I was often by myself when I didn't want to be, and I became acutely aware of feeling lonely as I grew older.

As a child, I learned to enjoy the time I had to myself. At least it was harmonious, and I didn't have to fear for my safety. I spent hours playing school or with my Barbie Dolls. I used my imagination to create the type of life I wished I were living; one filled with a loving, attentive family. Reading also took me away from my current situation and I would spend hours engrossed in any book I could get my hands on. I was such an avid reader, I quickly consumed all the books in our children's library, moving on to the teen and adult sections at an early age. I loved escaping from my life into every story I read.

In the summer, I spent many hours laying in the grass in our backyard, looking for images in the fluffy, white clouds and watching planes fly high in the sky overheard. With a mixture of awe and longing, I would fantasize about where the people were going but I never imagined I would have the opportunity to fly on a plane. Travel was a luxury that poor folks like my family could not afford.

My loneliness extended to activities outside of home. When I was in the fifth grade, I made the cheerleading squad for our basketball team. I was so excited I had been chosen. I really wanted to be a cheerleader, but I didn't think I had much of a chance. Going into the tryouts, my skills weren't remarkable. I was struggling with one critical jump I just couldn't accomplish. During tryouts,

I nailed the jump with perfection, landing a coveted spot on the squad. I rushed home feeling proud and happy, only to be met with anger from my mom. She was upset that we would need to buy special tennis shoes and socks to match the uniform supplied by the school. Her reaction definitely burst my bubble but did not entirely dim my pride in becoming a cheerleader.

Our school was small and didn't have a gym, so we were bussed to neighboring schools for the nighttime basketball games. On game days, I would hurry home to do my paper route, finish my homework, eat dinner, and change into my cheerleading uniform. Once ready, I would rush back to the school to catch the bus with the other cheerleaders and the basketball teams. It was so much fun to be at the games cheering on our team with my friends, but I always felt an underlying sense of loneliness. I was a cheerleader for two years and my parents never once attended a game to watch me cheer.

After the games, the bus returned to the school around 9 p.m. Other parents met the bus to pick up their kids, but mine never showed up. My dad would be asleep or passed out long before then and my mom rarely left the house at night. Sometimes my sister came to meet me, but most of the time I walked home alone in the cold, dark night, scared to death of what might be lurking in the shadows. The path home was especially scary at night, with dark railroad tracks, an open field, thick woods, few houses, and several unlit spots. I was usually the only person on the street. Inevitably, something would spook me, causing me to run like the dickens to my house, panting heavily as I opened the front door.

When I was twelve, I was admitted to the hospital with a very serious case of the flu. I loved the attention I got from the nurses during my weeklong stay. Even though I was sick, I was in heaven! I had three square meals a day and people regularly asked about my well-being. I didn't want to leave. When the doctor checked on me each day, I sat in fear that she would tell me this would be the day I could go home. I was so sad when she told me I would be discharged the next day. I didn't want to go home, I wanted to stay! I felt more love and caring from the nurses in the hospital than I did at home.

My dad picked me up at the hospital the morning I was discharged. We drove home in silence before he dropped me off at home and returned to work. When I entered the house, my mom was watching TV in the living room and didn't look up to greet me or inquire about my health. I ran directly upstairs to my room and cried for a long time, sobbing deeply in despair. I wanted to go back to the hospital where I was cared for and felt love.

Like many kids, Christmas was my favorite time of the year. My family had the tradition of celebrating it on Christmas Eve. We had a fake tree we assembled every year in our living room, and we strung shiny garland from one corner of the ceiling to another. I loved the excitement of the season and anticipating what Santa might bring for me. Even though we were poor, my parents always made sure we had a few presents under the tree.

The year I was twelve, my parents were not in the mood to celebrate Christmas and decided not to put up our decorations. I loved Christmas decorations and was adamant that we at least put up our tree. No one else wanted to help so, by myself, I lugged our fake tree and boxes of ornaments down from the attic. I assembled the tree, haphazardly strung the lights from top to bottom, and placed the ornaments on the branches. It was a lonely exercise but, in the end, I was happy to have some evidence that Christmas was on its way.

We didn't get as many presents that year and our gift exchange on Christmas Eve lasted ten minutes at most. We spent hardly any time together, following none of our traditions. In past years when the weather was mild, my dad drove us up to Chicago to see the beautiful Christmas lights and colorful decorations displayed throughout the city. That year, he did not even hint at the possibility of going. Instead, he fell asleep in his chair in the living room right after we opened our presents. Looking back, I realize that my parents had become very depressed but, at age twelve, I was not able to fully understand the state of their mental health.

We had a nice celebration the Christmas following my dad's death since my mom had the insurance money from his death to spend on gifts. My nephew, Christopher, had just been born in September and there is nothing like the joy of a baby to bring out the holiday spirit in all. Sadly, that was the last year we celebrated any holiday.

After my sister moved out, it was just me, my brother, and my mom. She was no longer cooking and had no money to spend on gifts. When I was fifteen, my mom handed me a pair of socks and said Merry Christmas before turning back to watch TV. There were no decorations to put up because they had been destroyed by the rats in the attic. When I was sixteen, she gave me the silent treatment all day, not responding when I said Merry Christmas to her.

I grew to dread all holidays. Cheryl didn't come home after she moved out, and my brother was either getting stoned in his room or out partying with friends. My friends were all busy with their families and none of our relatives extended an offer for us to join them. I sat alone in my room, trying to find something to occupy my time while the minutes slowly ticked by. I had no TV and, back then, there were no computers or personal devices to pass the time.

To this day, I feel very sad and lonely if I have to spend any time by myself on a holiday. My mom died in early December, seventeen days before Christmas. When the anniversary of her death comes each year, I am always overcome with the sadness of missing her and what might have been.

My greatest joy after my dad died was the birth of my nephew, Christopher. I loved this beautiful baby more than anything, and I was so happy that he and Cheryl were living with us. On the day he came home from the hospital, my sister had to go somewhere with Christopher's dad. My mom and I volunteered to take care of Christopher so he could rest undisturbed.

My mom was in a depressed mood, so I ended up watching Christopher alone, until my sister returned home later that night. I was barely thirteen years old, taking care of a five-day old baby! I had watched babies before in my babysitting jobs, but it was my first time alone with a newborn. Christopher's crib was in Cheryl's room, and I laid on her bed with him cuddled on my chest for hours. I felt unconditional love for the first time in my life. I had never known a love so pure and easy before.

While they lived at home, my life revolved around Christopher. I rushed home to play with and care for him after school. Being sixteen at the time, my sister had an active social life, so I ended up babysitting him often on school nights. I would sometimes hear him crying in her room when I was getting ready for school in the morning. Cheryl would still be sleeping, having been out late the night before. My mom ignored the crying so I would get him out of his crib, change his diaper, and feed him breakfast before heading off to school. If I had time, I also bathed him so he could go back into his crib freshly clean and with a full belly.

Eventually, Cheryl couldn't take my mom any longer and found a roommate to share a house. She and Christopher moved out before he was one year old. It was devastating for me. Not only was I losing the loving presence of Christopher in my life every day, but I also had no one to defend me from my mom. Deep loneliness set in.

After they left, our house was so quiet when my mom wasn't on a yelling tirade. I rarely had anyone to talk to when I was home. Even when my mom was in a normal mood, she and I never really clicked. She didn't put much effort into developing a relationship with me as she did with my sister. They could hang out and talk, but conversations between my mom and me were often awkward and strained. We didn't have a lot in common and I didn't trust her. Things I said to her when we were getting along were later twisted and used against me.

I made it a point to visit Christopher and Cheryl every chance I got. I would walk, have a friend drive me, or ride my bike to their house even though it was miles away in a different town. However, Cheryl got married when she was seventeen and they moved downstate Illinois when Christopher was about one and a half years old. When Cheryl, her husband, and Christopher came to our house to say goodbye, Christopher didn't want to leave me. He was clinging to me so tightly they had to pry him away from me while we hugged good-bye. When they drove off, Christopher's crying face was plastered against the back window of the pickup truck as he watched me standing there and I felt my heart being ripped out of my chest. With Cheryl and Christopher moving so far away, I felt absolutely alone for the first time in my life.

Until I learned how to deal with the feelings of loneliness, I mostly made bad decisions to try to counteract being lonely. When I let my guard down, I lacked discernment in friends and in romantic relationships. Unsurprisingly, I tended to attract people with narcissistic tendencies. My fear of being alone and my lack of self-worth, combined with having been raised by a narcissistic mother, made me a perfect target for energy vampires - people who are willing to be with you as long as you do what they want and act how they want you to act. People who preyed on my lack of self-worth also contributed to lowering it to keep me under their control. There were many highs and lows with these people but rarely much satisfaction for me.

I felt so happy when someone actually wanted to be with me that I put myself second to their wishes. I often put aside my needs and wants to go along with whatever the other person wanted to do – even when I had no interest in it and would rather be doing something else. This became such a habit that I stopped pursuing what I wanted to do even when I was alone, or on the rare occasion when someone asked me what I wanted to do. I stopped believing I was worthy of pursuing my own interests.

As I healed, I became aware of how my mom's advice to "stop being so smart so people will like you" contributed to my dysfunctional, co-dependent, relationships and set the standard for me to put others' wishes before my own. I have come to see that loneliness really stems from not knowing our True Self and the power we have within us. We are cut off from the loving, powerful creative beings we truly are. We forget that we are deeply connected with everyone and everything on this planet.

As I travel on my path to knowing my True Self, I realize I can choose whether to feel lonely or not. In this life we are never alone. We are supported and loved by God. No matter what you do in this life, you will always be supported. Life is a learning experience for expansion. When you heal all the negativity and pain within you and replace it with love and light, you will begin to feel your True Self. You will feel joyful and have inner peace most of the time. You will attract circumstances and people that reflect this new marvelous, magnificent version of you. And you will be a beacon of light for others, showing them that the impossible is possible.

24

MY (NOT SO GOOD) APPROACH TO FRIENDSHIP

━━━ ♥ ━━━

My hometown was like any other rural town in the Midwest; quaint homes, a small downtown area, lots of taverns and churches, and surrounded by cornfields and farms. When I was a child, we moved six times by the time I was twelve years old. The longest we lived in one spot was for almost seven years in a two-story house located on the main street of the town. The house was old, decrepit, and drafty. When I was seven years old, the city deemed the house no longer habitable and officially condemned it. We had to quickly pack up and go. I was sad about moving, since we had lived there since I was a baby. I loved my second-grade teacher at my elementary school, I knew my way around the neighborhood, and I had several friends my age who lived within blocks of us.

We moved to the other side of town, into a house my dad's brother had bought to fix up and sell. The whole property was in poor condition, the yard untended with a huge junk pile taking up much of the space. Among the mess was an old, dilapidated '50s pickup truck my dad tried unsuccessfully to get running; a tattered dresser that had a bunch of old, yellow human teeth in the top drawer; and a broken refrigerator, the door of which my dad removed so my sister and I wouldn't accidentally get trapped. I moved to a new school to finish second grade, slowly making friends during this transition.

When my parents got divorced the next year, my dad's brother made us move out of the house. There was no love lost between my mom and my dad's family, just like my mom's family didn't care much for my dad. Even though she had just won $10,000 on a scratcher in the Illinois State Lottery, my mom moved us into another condemned house just a short distance away. Today, I cannot fathom why she didn't move us into a nicer, safer home but at the time, I didn't think much about it. I was just happy that this time I was able to stay at the same school with my new friends.

After my parents got remarried, they used my mom's lottery winnings to buy a house in a nearby small town. I was nine years old when we moved from my hometown and it was a tough move for both me and Cheryl. The town was closely-knit and unwelcoming to new residents. We always felt like outsiders, never quite fitting in, often picked on and bullied by other kids. Three years later, when I was twelve, with a huge sigh of relief we moved back to my hometown. That happiness was short-lived, however, because my dad committed suicide only eight months later.

As happy as I was to move back, it was another difficult transition for me. I had become used to a small school that housed kindergarten through eighth grade, where my class was made up of fifteen or so kids. I was now attending a junior high fed by three different elementary

MY (NOT SO GOOD) APPROACH TO FRIENDSHIP

schools. The size seemed enormously overwhelming and I didn't remember most of the kids I was friends with when I lived there earlier.

Given my family dynamics and our unstable home life, creating new relationships was not easy for me. Guarded and cautious, I definitely didn't want other kids to know what went on at my house. Expecting everyone to be as unpredictable and threatening as my family was, I was afraid of being seen by anyone. The volatility at home made me feel prone to hiding who I was and playing it safe in most social situations. Repeatedly moving schools after the start of the school year and being put in the excruciatingly vulnerable position of making new friends, just compounded the shyness. It took months until I started to feel safe in a new environment with new people. Only when I got to know and trust someone did I really open up and be myself.

Ultimately, I was my own downfall when it came to cultivating lasting and loving friendships as a child. To be blunt, I wasn't always a good friend. I didn't intend it to be this way, I didn't really know any better. Living in a constant state of lack, I was envious of what others had, be it friends, cars, parents, clothes, money, or happiness. I grew up believing relationships worked the way my mom treated us. I often emulated her behavior of talking about people and choosing favorites, getting one friend to not like another because I was jealous. I was controlling and manipulative, and I learned it from the master.

My mom spared no one when she was on a rant. She gossiped about my friends to me and she was extremely judgmental about these children. She told me which ones I should like, who she liked better than me, and who she thought were losers. She loved to stress the ones she felt were superior to me, going over in great detail the reasons why. Sometimes she told me she wished they were her daughter instead of me. I would end up feeling threatened by my friends and lash out at them, using her tactics. I am sure they were confused, since they were completely unaware of how she was manipulating me.

Many of my friendships in my younger life ended up broken due to my behavior. As an adult, I became conscious of this behavior and was able to overcome it. Learning about how the Ego Mind works and developing the ability to watch my thoughts allowed me to stop unconsciously shifting into this negative behavior. Presence is the key to really seeing how manipulative our Ego Minds can be. The result is that I am respectful and loving to others, and so my friendships today are also respectful and loving.

25

MY RELATIONSHIP WITH MY SISTER

Growing up, my hero was my older sister, Cheryl. I was in awe of her. I thought she could do anything and that she knew everything. She was super-smart and did really well in school. We had what I'd like to think was a normal sister relationship when we were kids, at least as much as we could have in our family. We played together and we fought with each other. Her three-year-old self wasn't happy when I came along. Our mom later told stories of Cheryl being mad at her after she came home from the hospital with me. I'm sure it wasn't easy having our parents' attention stolen by a new baby in the house.

Our parents treated us differently and put very distinct labels on us. Cheryl was the responsible and mature one, I was the cute and helpless one. Because we had so little money, Cheryl had to wear hand-me-downs from one of our male cousins. I was too small and skinny to fit in the boy hand-me-downs, so I was given girls clothes from yard sales or the Kmart clearance rack. My dad must have wanted a boy because he cut my sister's hair so short that everyone mistook her for one, especially when she was wearing our cousin's clothes. I was allowed to let my hair grow long. While these were my parent's decisions, none of this put me in Cheryl's good graces.

My mom relied on Cheryl to cook and do housework from a very young age. I wasn't assigned chores but sometimes I was given a dime to help my mom with the dishes. This made Cheryl very upset because she didn't get any reward for helping. Other times, when I wanted to help, I was told I was too young and didn't do it right. "Just get out of the way," was the message I often heard. I am sure that to Cheryl this came across as favoritism toward me, but it really made me feel I wasn't capable. Years later, I felt I had to work extra hard to prove myself as more than the cute and helpless one.

My mom also made Cheryl take care of me from a very early age, which caused Cheryl to resent me even more. I don't blame her for it; my mom was passing her adult responsibilities on to a little kid. Yet Cheryl also chose to step in from time to time to protect me from my parents when they were out of control. When she felt brave and we were getting along, she hid me when my dad came home drunk or defended me when my mom was picking on me. She sometimes met me at the school at night to walk me home after the basketball games so I wouldn't have to be alone in the dark. I looked to her as my female role model. If I wanted advice about anything or when something momentous happened in my life, I always went to Cheryl first.

Cheryl and I shared a bedroom during the early years of our childhood. The old, drafty house on 4th Street had only one furnace that heated the downstairs; our bedroom upstairs did not have a direct vent. We dreaded bedtime in the winter, the frigid air stinging our bare skin as we quickly changed from our clothes into our PJs. Cheryl and I shared a small bed in our tiny room. We rushed under the covers, making snow angel movements with our arms and legs, using the friction to quickly warm up the sheets. I had a hard time falling asleep when my feet were ice-cold, and I begged Cheryl to let me put my feet on her back to warm them up. She didn't like it and would say no several times but, in the end, she always gave in.

When I was ten, my mom told me and Cheryl that if we wanted anything outside of the school clothes she bought once a year, we had to buy it ourselves. To earn the spending money we needed, both Cheryl and I started delivering newspapers every day after school and on Saturdays. We walked or biked the paper routes all year long – winter, spring, summer, and fall. It didn't matter if it was sunny, rainy, windy, or snowing – we were out there delivering the papers on time.

The winters of those years went on record as blizzard winters. We headed out on our paper routes immediately after school and did not arrive home until after dark, our bodies feeling frozen from head to toe. The clothes and boots we wore were insufficient for below-zero temperatures and the accompanying wind, ice, and snow. My feet became so numb that I could no longer feel my flesh, and every painful step felt like I was walking on brittle bones. Once home, Cheryl and I huddled up over the heating vents, crying at the pain we felt as our frozen bodies started thawing out.

It was no wonder I would reach out to Cheryl when my relationship with my mom took a turn for the worse. Cheryl was the only other person on the planet who really knew what I was going through, having escaped it herself. Growing up the way we did left us with many demons to overcome and we took them out on each other in different ways. Our relationship experienced many ups and downs until I moved to California when I was 27. Today, we stay in contact, checking in on each other from time to time. But on our different life journeys, we do not have a close relationship.

I used to be judgmental of Cheryl in her decisions and actions. At the time, I thought I was being loving because I always felt she could do better than what she was doing. As I grow in my spiritual journey in knowing my True Self, I have begun to see her as her True Self. This has allowed me to forgive her and myself for the parts of our relationship that were not aligned to love, and to feel love for her True Self.

26

TRUE-SELF EXERCISE

♥

Method: Meditation

Meditation is a powerful way to align your energy back to love. As your mind quiets, you fall into a calm state and are ready to hear divine messages from within.

I studied meditation and learned there are many different practices, each with different guidelines. I found the different styles to be complicated and confusing for the average person. Instead, I prefer to follow a very simple method, one that can be done sitting, standing, or lying down.

How to practice Meditation:

1. As with all the other techniques, start by "Connect to Your Heart Space."
2. Keep your eyes closed while breathing in and out in a normal pattern.

3. Keep your attention on your breath. Use it to anchor you into the present moment.
4. When thoughts arise, observe them but do not attach to them.
5. Practice for as long as you can.
6. Sometimes, before starting a meditation, I will ask my True Self for guidance to a situation I am dealing with, or for something new I want to pursue. I may ask for guidance on how to deal with one of my daughters, or what the next step is in a current endeavor. The answer may show up during the meditation or it may come to me later that day or the next. I just need to be open to receiving it in whatever way it may come. The next chapter shows the good that can happen when you become open to help from others.

27

KINDNESS OF STRANGERS

♥

I experienced not having a home twice in my life, and each time I relied on the kindness of strangers to give me a roof over my head. After my mom died, Cheryl was the only relative in my life. While I had aunts, uncles, and cousins on both sides of the family, I had no relationship with them. My mom had stopped talking to her family when she became severely depressed and my dad's family did not remain in touch with us after his mom died when I was fifteen.

The first time I had no place to call home, I was eighteen. After our mom died, I continued to live with Cheryl until just after I turned eighteen. For much of the time we lived together, I babysat my nephew, Christopher, who was then four, and my niece, Sarah, who was two, while Cheryl went to work.

Once again, I had Christopher blessing me with the gift of unconditional love when I needed it most. But this time, I was now receiving double the love with Sarah in my life. Sarah was born after Cheryl and her then-husband moved to downstate Illinois, so we really started our relationship when I moved in with them. As with Christopher, it was love at first sight with Sarah. I really adored taking care of them and doing my best to make sure their needs were met. We developed a close bond that still exists today.

When we lived together, Cheryl and I had both good times and bad times while we tried to deal with the trauma of our mom dying without any outside support. We drank a lot of beer on some nights, listening to music, and crying our hearts out. Sometimes we fought with each other, other times we consoled each other. When we didn't want to drink beer, we pulled out our mom's favorite teapot that we saved from her house after she died. We spent hours drinking black tea while playing euchre, our favorite card game that was hugely popular in the Midwest at the time. I think we acted sillier from the tea than we did from drinking beer and we always had a good time.

I was able to land a short-term job at the local library through funding available to teenagers from low-income families. I loved that job and all the ladies I worked with. Given my appreciation for reading, it gave me so much joy to work with books every day. I found great pleasure in preparing new books to be lent out and filing the books the patrons returned back to shelves per the Dewey Decimal System. I had the opportunity to gain valuable skills working on the computer. Unfortunately, the funding was limited, and I was not able to continue working there once I turned eighteen. Finding a new job was not easy. I didn't have many marketable skills and I didn't have a driver's license. Just after I turned eighteen, I was unemployed, and my Social Security benefits had expired.

Being new to the Chicago area, it was not easy for me to meet people my own age. I had little opportunity to interact with other teenagers since I spent most of my time at the library or at home. Mary, my friend from my hometown, would come visit every chance she could, and we explored the local teen hangouts. This is where I met my new friend, Michelle.

A couple of months after I turned eighteen, I was out with Michelle, and we stopped at Cheryl's townhouse so I could pick up a shirt I wanted to wear that night. Cheryl's new boyfriend stopped me in the living room and told me I could no longer live there. He had recently moved in with Cheryl and he didn't want me there now that I wasn't bringing in any money. He said I had to move out right then and there. He gave me no notice, just an order to get out now. Where would I go? I barely knew anyone here! *This couldn't be true; my own sister wouldn't do this to me*, I thought. "Are you in agreement with this?" I asked Cheryl and she affirmed it was true. I was in shock that my sister, who had saved me from my mom less than a year ago, was now telling me to move out of her house without any warning.

Michelle said I could stay with her and, not knowing what else to do, I packed up whatever belongings I could grab. While I was grateful I had a place to go, I didn't want to stay at Michelle's house. She was fun but controlling and somewhat narcissistic. Her home life was volatile, with two alcoholic parents who became violent when they drank, which was often. My only other choice was to live on the street, so I stayed at her house.

It was hell for me, almost worse than being at home with my mom because I was not part of this family. Michelle desperately wanted me to be there with her. I am sure it gave her a sense of safety to have me there when her parents fought.

My former boss at the library learned of my plight and let me come stay with her and her husband. She was instrumental in helping me get back on my feet and providing a sense of stability in my life. While I lived with them, I was able to get my GED, my driver's license, a car, and a steady job. She helped me to create a solid baseline so that I could move forward towards success. I will always be grateful for that much needed support given to me in my time of need.

At the time, I felt the ultimate betrayal from Cheryl. Today, looking back, I am sure she wanted to rid herself of the burden of a teenager who needed more than she could give. Cheryl had her own set of challenges, having just gone through a divorce with two young children. I also discovered that moving out of her place was probably the best thing to happen for my future and my ability to take care of myself.

The next time I had nowhere to live was when I was evicted from my apartment when I was twenty-one. I didn't know how to manage money and I could not pay the rent. I was delinquent on credit-card debt and had a very low credit rating. I was working full time, making a little more than the minimum wage of $3.35. I had also begun a rigorous college program that required me to pay for the books and tuition that student loans didn't cover. To say money was tight was an understatement.

It was tough for me to find a new apartment due to my lack of financial merit. Having nowhere to go, I piled my clothes and the other items I used daily into my car. I rented a small storage unit for my furniture and dishes. I began sleeping on friend's couches, sometimes not knowing where I might find a place to crash until late in the day. I had stayed close with a former boyfriend's mom, and she offered me a room in their basement when I told her about my situation. Relieved at having some stability, even for the short-term, I gratefully took her up on the offer.

While it provided a roof over my head, it was an uncomfortable month. I loved being with her, but I am sure my ex-boyfriend, his dad, and his brother did not want me there. I felt like an unwelcome intruder. Fortunately, with my work and college class schedule I was rarely around, and in my free time I actively looked for an alternative place to live.

I looked everywhere but there were few housing options within my limited financial range. A guy from one of my college classes was looking for a roommate. I had no other option, so I took him up on his offer. It turned out to be a huge mistake. As a student, he also couldn't afford much rent and lived in a low-income complex. Men congregated outside during all hours of the day and night, drinking beer and harassing other residents. They would either greet me with catcalls or silently stare me down when I left my car and walked to the apartment. Some of the men stood by our front door when I was home alone. They never knocked, but I found their presence intimidating and I feared having to leave if they were lurking outside the apartment. After one week, I started looking for a new place to live.

I couldn't find any apartments that fit my budget, so I decided to look for a room to rent. At first, I resisted the idea of living in someone else's house again, but it was really my only option. I found a room in a family's home and, while I wouldn't have the freedoms I was used to, it provided a safe and secure environment. I stayed with them for about two years and while they were nice, I felt uncomfortable much of the time I lived with them. The feeling of being an intruder remained with me the entire time I was there.

I went on to rent a room from my friend Kate's mom, Donna, and stayed there for my last two years of college. I love them both and really enjoyed the time I lived with Donna. I mostly felt like I was part of their family unit and I belonged. Still, there was a small part of me that always felt like an interloper. This feeling would not go away until I moved to California and my then-husband and I rented an apartment of our own. To this day, I still feel uncomfortable staying at people's houses to the point that when I am traveling, I prefer to be at a hotel where I can have my own space on my own terms.

28

FROM HIGH SCHOOL DROPOUT TO COLLEGE GRADUATE

———— ♥ ————

Schoolwork came easily to me; the social aspect of school did not. As I progressed through junior high and high school, my confidence in myself and my abilities significantly declined. After my dad died, it became harder for me to go to school. I was allowed to stay home the week of his death but was sent back to school the following Monday like nothing had happened. I was not given grief counseling and I don't recall my teachers talking to me about what happened. My friends were supportive when I first returned to school, but twelve-year-old's have a short attention span for anything outside of themselves. Life went on as usual for everyone else, but I still had all this pain stuck in me.

When I was thirteen, my mom's emotional outbursts began happening more frequently in the morning, leaving me drained and anxious before school even started. On those days, I had a hard time focusing, and my teachers would reprimand me in front of the entire class when I was caught daydreaming. It was embarrassing and I became even more withdrawn.

My eighth-grade graduation was a day of heartache. I was so excited to be finishing junior high as it was the most important milestone I had achieved in my young life to date. I don't even remember why it started, but my mom went on one of her tirades that lasted for hours, exclaiming she wasn't going to my graduation. I had wronged her somehow and she said I didn't deserve her to be there. Putting herself on the line, Cheryl got involved to defend me and the three of us began fighting.

I cried and pleaded with my mom over and over to come but she refused to give in. I was a mess when it came time to get ready for the event with puffy eyes, a tearstained face, and a red nose. I had been so excited about wearing the beautiful new dress my dad's mom had bought for me, and the pretty high heels I had begged my mom to buy. I felt so worn down I didn't even want to put them on. Cheryl took me upstairs and helped me get ready while our mom continued to yell at us. It was just Cheryl and baby Christopher who walked with me to the school, Cheryl consoling me the whole way.

I felt out of place when we got there. The auditorium was full of my classmates' parents and family members who had come to watch them receive their diplomas. People were buzzing around in excitement and joy. Cheryl and I decided on a place to meet after the ceremony. She had offered to take home my cap, gown, and diploma so I wouldn't have to bring them to the class dance that was happening immediately after. She and Christopher found a seat while I joined my class for the processional through the auditorium.

FROM HIGH SCHOOL DROPOUT TO COLLEGE GRADUATE

The ceremony went by in a blur. I couldn't stop thinking about the fight with my mom and that I had no parents there to see me graduate. I felt lonely and it still hurt me greatly that my dad had died the previous year. When my name was called, I walked across the stage to shake our principal's hand when I was awarded my diploma. After the ceremony ended, we filed out of the auditorium the same way we came in. I almost stopped in my tracks when I saw my mom sitting in the aisle seat of one of the last rows. I looked at her expectantly, hoping for a smile or some positive recognition, but she just glared back at me and looked away.

I met Cheryl and Christopher in the school lobby. We stood there for a while, feeling awkward while families congregated around us, taking pictures and congratulating their graduates. We couldn't afford a camera to take pictures. We looked for our mom, but we did not see her again at the school. Cheryl and Christopher soon left, taking my cap, gown and diploma with them. I went to the graduation dance in the school gym and waited for my friends as they freed up from their family photos. That night, I was able to forget about my mom while I had fun dancing and laughing with my friends. It was probably the last time in my life I felt like a kid, young and carefree.

Even with all the challenges of my home life and spending a lot of time taking care of Christopher, I still managed to graduate from junior high with high grades and was enrolled in honors classes when I entered my freshman year in high school.

Freshman year was uneventful. I really don't recall much about it. I must have done well because I once again made it into honors classes in my sophomore year. However, my whole life had changed that summer and

I was a very different person when I started school that fall. As my mom's mental health deteriorated and I started taking on the responsibilities of the house, it became harder for me to go to school. I was in a constant state of anxiety about the situation at home, and socially I couldn't relate to most kids my age.

When I came back to school in my sophomore year, my friends from junior high started ignoring me, going so far as to turn their backs on me when I walked up to the group before the first morning bell. When I approached their lunch table, either I was ignored during the conversation or there was no place for me to sit. They wouldn't tell me why I was no longer welcome. It hurt my feelings, so I stopped going around them.

Too shy to easily make new friends, I didn't know many other kids at school, and I often spent lunch hours sitting by myself in the crowded cafeteria. One day in homeroom, one of the girls in the friend group told me they didn't want to be around me anymore because I acted old, and they just wanted to have fun. I was too serious and a bummer to be around. It was painful to hear but I knew it was a true assessment of who I had become.

At that point, I was already gravitating toward people who were older than me, many of them out of school and usually also from highly dysfunctional family situations. I attracted people like me, those who didn't have a good home life and wanted to escape their problems. The rural area I grew up in didn't fare well economically in the '70s and '80s and it proved to be a breeding ground for dysfunctional families. You could say most of my friends were part of the "burnout" crowd, although many of us didn't do drugs.

We did like to drink though, mostly beer at someone's house whose parents were not home. We didn't always make the best choices in what we did and how we acted toward others. We were a bunch of kids who were all hurting and trying to find our way without much adult supervision. We were growing up too fast for our own good. I started hanging out with my friends until late at night, not getting up for school the next morning.

Going to school became more difficult and it was becoming harder to concentrate on the subjects. Math or science didn't mean that much to me when I was worried about my safety at home and my most basic needs were not being met. I couldn't bear to be around other "normal" kids at school, kids who seemed to have no cares.

School was so unbearable for me that I did everything I could to avoid it. I often tried to convince my mom I was sick so I could stay home, which rarely worked. Even so, it was not uncommon for me to play hooky from several classes or not show up for an entire day without an excuse from her. As punishment, I spent many days in in-school detention, causing me to miss even more days of class.

My mom lied to the school administrators when they talked to her about my truancy. She told them that I was responsible for all the problems at home and that she could not control me. Like a true narcissist, she was adept at painting herself as the victim instead of the perpetrator. My mom was so convincing in her lies that the school administrators believed her stories over my account of our home situation. There was talk of sending me to live in a juvenile detention center but, ultimately, their only punishment was to expel me from school.

I was kicked out of school both semesters of my sophomore and junior years. I was so far behind I didn't even try to go back my senior year. In hindsight, it wouldn't have mattered if I had stayed in school. My escape to my sister's in November of that year would have forced me to drop out. While most kids my age were excitedly planning for college and their futures, I was coping with issues of survival and the loss of my mom.

When I did attend school, I got good grades. I could miss classes, yet still pass tests with decent scores. To some, it looked like I was throwing away a promising future. Meaning well, my homeroom teacher lectured me, telling me that if I didn't continue in school, I would amount to nothing. I told him he didn't know what was really going on at my house. I said that just because I was going through a lot of challenges, it didn't mean it would stop me from becoming something later in my life. Even during that dark period of my life, the light of my True Self was there inside me. There was a hope and a belief in a better future.

And that better future was coming. I was able to shift my life by listening to my True Self. At the time, I didn't know what the voice was, but I heard it and felt it so powerfully that I knew I had to act. I've learned that once God speaks through you, you need to quickly take inspired action to create what it is you want.

I was twenty-one and in a dead-end job as a waitress. I was a job-hopper up to that point, having worked at an office supply store, three different hotels, a supermarket, and a gas station in only three years. One morning while getting ready for work, I had an awakening. I heard the voice of my True Self telling me I was supposed to do more with my life. I felt it in my heart, a calling to stop playing small. I knew that only I could create a bigger life for myself. No one else was going to do the work to make my life better.

But how was I going to do this? What could I do? I thought of several career options before landing on the field of computer technology. I wasn't sure exactly what I could do, since my experience was limited mostly to data entry. But I liked working on computers and quickly became an expert user of the computer systems at all my jobs.

I was first introduced to computers at the library, where I logged all the new books into the system catalog and created small databases for special projects. At age 18, I was working as a front desk supervisor of a resort hotel when I was first exposed to the inner workings of computers. When our front desk system went down, it was my responsibility to work with the company who built it. Their system administrators instructed me on the corrections to make in the application code, and I would boot the system back up. I loved fixing the problems and seeing the immediate results in action.

Everyone I worked with encouraged me to go to college and pursue a career in computers. Cheryl's boyfriend at the time had graduated from DeVry Institute of Technology (today known as DeVry University) and had a successful career in electronics. He felt strongly that I should check it out and I figured I had nothing to lose by applying.

I was pretty good at taking tests, so the entrance exam requirements did not intimidate me. When I was 18, I had passed the GED with high scores, finishing much faster than the others testing with me. The school administrator personally came out to congratulate me on my results, emphasizing that I must go to college.

As I expected, I easily passed the entrance exam at DeVry, and within a few months I was attending college at night. I landed a full-time clerical job with Raytheon, whose tuition reimbursement package helped pay some of my school bills. The Universe was lining up everything I needed to succeed.

For the next four years and eight months, I was on a mission to get my Bachelor of Science degree and nothing was going to get in my way. When I first started college, my friends at the time laughed at me. They couldn't conceive of me going to college for such a complex subject. I can see where they were coming from, since our common bond was going out drinking and dancing at clubs on the weekends. None of them were pursuing anything meaningful of their own. I wasn't about to let their limiting beliefs get in my way, so I decided it was time to get new friends. It was lonely for a while, but I began meeting people at DeVry with whom I had more in common.

DeVry was an environment in which I could thrive socially. Going to school at night meant my other classmates were also full-time workers, many of whom were working toward a second career. Almost everyone was older than me and I felt comfortable around them. I don't think I could have ever been successful in the typical college experience of living in a dorm and joining a sorority, given how difficult it was for me to connect with most people my own age.

I was dedicated to seeing my education through, no matter what it took. My biggest hurdle was finances since I had no one to help me shoulder the high cost of education. To pay for part of my tuition, I took out government student loans that did not require repayment until after graduation. My full-time job at Raytheon barely covered the remaining school costs and living expenses. To get extra money, I often worked on weekends as a cocktail waitress at various restaurants and bars.

Living in the suburbs with little public transportation required a reliable car to get me back and forth from home to work and school. Unfortunately, the best I could afford was an old car that broke down on a regular basis. I couldn't always pay for the repairs, so I learned tips and tricks to get around them. For example, the car needed a new alternator, but I needed to save up money to fix it. As luck would have it, it was the height of winter. While sitting outside overnight in the bitter cold, the car battery would completely drain, causing the car to not start in the morning. I needed to leave at 6:30am to be at work by 7:30am, so there was little room to deal with a car that wouldn't start.

To combat this, every weeknight I got up in the middle of the night, got dressed, went out in the subzero temperatures to start the car and let it run for 10 minutes. Once the battery was adequately recharged, I could return to the warm house and sleep for a few more hours before my alarm went off at 5:30am. This was the only way I could ensure a running car every day in the winter. I sure was thankful when I had saved up the funds I needed and was able to have the alternator replaced!

I had high delinquent credit card debt to deal with, and I vowed to pay it back in its entirety to the collection agencies. When I started school, I clearly had no idea how to handle my money, but I knew if I didn't pay that debt off, I would never forgive myself. I had started taking my word seriously and I would not go back on the commitment to repay the money I borrowed. I was accountable for how I used the money and repaying it to the bank was my responsibility, no one else's.

Putting myself on a strict budget, I was able to pay off every single penny of the debt within a couple years. My hard work at Raytheon was also paying off and I was seeing raises and promotions on a regular basis. I now had good credit and I celebrated this victory with purchasing my first brand-new car. Even though it was a small, inexpensive car, I can't even begin to describe the joy and sense of accomplishment I felt the day I drove it off the car dealer's lot.

My job at Raytheon was in the document-control center of the nuclear engineering department and the work was mostly tedious. There was a great amount of paperwork to fill out and there was a never-ending pile of project documents and blueprints to file.

To pass the time while doing the repetitive tasks I daydreamed, happily visualizing myself in my new technology career once I graduated from DeVry. I imagined myself happy and successful as an executive leader at a major corporation. I pictured my mannerisms, the clothes I would wear, and what the offices looked like.

I didn't know it at the time, but I was creating my future through visualization. During my career, I have held technical and executive positions at successful major corporations including The Walt Disney Company, Hyatt Hotels, and Universal Music Group.

The setbacks I faced along the way, like high debt and homelessness, did not stop me from reaching my vision of graduating college. After four years and eight months of dedicated focus, I graduated Summa Cum Laude from DeVry with a Bachelor of Science in Computer Information Systems. I started my technology career that same month.

29

TRUE-SELF EXERCISE

♥

Method: Gratitude

Gratitude is one of the most healing and attracting energies that exists. Gratitude is an easy way to shift your energy to align with your True Self. Gratitude puts you in the energy of love. You will create tremendous, positive, changes in your life by cultivating a practice of gratitude for yourself and for everything life brings to you.

When I look back at my life journey from a higher perspective, I feel grateful for the growth I experienced through the adversity of my early life and for my life as it stands today. Every day I practice gratitude for my health, for my daughters, for living in a near constant state of inner peace and calm, for living in a beautiful city blocks from the Pacific Ocean, for being employed, for having a good relationship with my ex-husband, for being able to provide for myself and my daughters, for the food on the table, for my mental and emotional health, for having loving relationships, and for having the wherewithal to deal with any situation that pops up. I am most grateful that I live in an almost constant state of inner peace and calm.

There are many ways to practice gratitude. When you say thank you, become present and feel it while you say it. When someone blesses you for sneezing, don't just say thank you absentmindedly. Instead, really feel it within yourself, and send the feeling of gratitude to the other person as you say thank you. When you get paid, don't feel despair if your paycheck doesn't cover all your bills. Send thanks for the money that is coming into your life today.

I love the old saying, "If you take care of the pennies, the dollars will take care of themselves." Whenever I find a penny on the ground, I celebrate it as though I just won millions in the lottery. View all the money you have coming into your life, no matter how much or how little, as a blessing and watch it multiply when you align to this loving energy.

Right now, I'd like you to take stock of your life and think about everything you should feel grateful for. At first, that may not be easy to do. It certainly wasn't for me. Our Ego Minds tend to focus on what's wrong and needs fixing. When you practice gratitude, I challenge you to include all aspects of your life, regardless of whether you judge them good or bad. As you look at what the mind has labeled bad through the eyes of gratitude, you may just see the blessing in it. Don't be surprised if this results in the healing of adverse situations as you begin to embody your True Self through the practice of gratitude.

How to Practice Gratitude:

It's best to do this exercise in the morning or in the evening. It's even better if you can do it both times, focusing on gratitude when you first wake up and right before you go to bed.

1. Begin with the "Connect to Your Heart Space" exercise.
2. Write down 10 things for which you are grateful.
3. Spend a few moments reading each line from your gratitude list out loud and invoke the feeling of gratitude in your body. Reading aloud while experiencing this positive feeling will begin to change your energy in positive ways, and soon you may notice a difference in what you attract into your world.
4. Practice gratitude multiple times throughout the day and really watch your life change in miraculous ways.
5. It's important to focus on gratitude with the energy of love. If you do this from a manipulative or spiteful place, your results will reflect that negative intention.

30

HEALTH AND HEALING MYSELF

———— ♥ ————

Health, along with money, is one of the most controversial topics when it comes to the ability to self-heal. Of the two, we often have more limiting beliefs when it comes to the idea of healing ourselves. Instead of seeing the gifts our physical being brings to us through the state of our health, we see our body as separate and often as an enemy against whom we must fight. As women, we are taught that our physical bodies must look a certain way and if they don't, we are defective. Western medicine has us fighting against our body constantly. We fight cancer and a variety of other diseases but in reality, we are only battling with ourselves.

What we resist, persists. When we fight a disease, we create a strong energetic vibration within ourselves that holds what we don't want in place. We come from a place of fear and there is enormous negative energy behind this "war" mindset. Our resistance will keep us in a place of illness if we do not allow our natural abilities to heal us.

I believe the physical ailments that show up in our body are blessings. These symptoms are showing us where we are out of alignment with our True Self, giving us an opportunity to come back into harmony with it. As infinite beings, we may come into this world sick or develop an illness when we are a child. These are decisions we made prior to coming here in order to experience expansion for our soul growth and for those around us.

Our body is an intelligent system, but we need to know how to read it. Each ailment, depending on where it occurs and what it is, gives you a hint of where you are out of alignment with love. It gives you an indication of where you need to shift beliefs to come back to your True Self.

There is much written about self-healing, and I encourage you to explore this topic for yourself. Some of my favorite books include:

- *Your Body's Telling You: Love Yourself!: The most complete book on metaphysical causes of illnesses and diseases* by Lisa Bourbeau
- *Heal Your Body* by Louise Hay
- *The Energy Codes: The 7-Step System to Awaken Your Spirit, Heal Your Body, and Live Your Best Life* by Dr. Sue Morten
- *The Healing Code: 6 Minutes to Heal the Source of Your Health, Success, or Relationship Issue* by Alexander Lloyd, PhD, ND

Healing yourself requires that you step away from fear and examine what is within you that is not aligned to love. Many people do not want to do this. They are afraid to discover what may be lurking within them, so they do not voluntarily explore this inner territory. It's easier to go to a doctor and put the job of curing you on them. We expect the experts to heal us using prescription drugs, surgery, radiation, and other techniques; when cures don't work, it's easier to place blame on the methods and the doctors instead of holding ourselves accountable for our health.

As the saying goes, *Incurable means curable from within.* There are countless stories of people curing themselves from terrible diseases by shifting their beliefs and using the energy of love. These aren't miracles that come from outside of ourselves. They come through us from within and we all can heal using our true power of divinity.

Aligning to my True Self has allowed me to maintain great health, which is opposite of what you might expect given my history. My parents had a slew of health problems including high blood pressure, arthritis, and heart disease. According to the ACE study, the amount of adversity I experienced as a child puts me at an increased risk for heart disease, stroke, cancer, and diabetes.

When my body is out of alignment, I can clear the pain by using the True-Self exercises I have included in this book. One particularly impactful example of how I healed myself happened over two years ago.

At the time, I was experiencing severe pain in my lower body for months on end. My hips were locked tight, my tailbone felt like it was on fire, and my lower back was as taut as a fully stretched rubber band. I also suffered from plantar fasciitis, a condition that causes deep heel pain. Running is a physical activity that brings me pure joy and I was sad that I could no longer run every day. Walking was difficult and I could barely bend over to put on my socks and shoes.

I tried chiropractic treatment, acupuncture, Yoga, stretching exercises, ice, heating pads, and over-the-counter pain medication with little success. I enrolled in a Pilates class and the exercises I did on the reformer provided only short-term relief. Friends chalked up my symptoms to "aging", saying that that my body was just getting old and stiff. I didn't see it that way.

I decided it was time to put my money where my mouth is and use the Release Technique to heal myself. As you can imagine, there were many layers to work through. My body provided many clues on where to start my healing. The hips represent how we are moving through life, either with ease or struggle. The lower back shows us our feelings related to the financial support we are receiving. The tailbone symbolizes stability, security, and basic needs being met.

I was at a point in my life where my finances were very tight. A very sudden and painful split in a relationship had recently altered my life direction. And deep within, I was carrying around the childhood traumas that made me feel unsafe and uncared for.

It took several sessions of the Release Technique combined with visualizing negative energy leaving my tailbone. I decided to go sit by the ocean for the last session. The ocean is a sacred space for me that represents calm and personal power. I love watching the waves as they roll in and out. To me, seagulls embody freedom and I always end up with a flock surrounding me wherever I sit. This time was no different.

During the session, while focusing on my heart space, I envisioned healing. The pain was so intense that even sitting on the sand was uncomfortable. During the Release Technique, I visualized the brilliant golden light breaking up the painful energy that was stuck within my body, freeing me from the blocks that were holding me back in life.

I sent love to myself, all the while observing what came up in my thoughts and feelings but not attaching to them.

When I finished my session, I hobbled back up the hill to my home. I went to bed early that night, feeling drained as the misaligned energy began to leave my body. At first, I thought I was coming down with a bug, but I realized that this was evidence that the Release Technique was working. I awoke the next morning to an entirely different feeling in my lower body. I had full motion in my back and hips allowing me to bend and sit easily. My heels felt loose and flexible when I walked from my bedroom to the kitchen. To this day, I no longer experience pain in those parts of my body.

My most recent healing was profound and came as a result of healing work I did with my life energy coaches. I had always bruised easily as far back as I can remember. Just lightly bumping into something could result in a massive mark on my body. I wasn't aware of how I got most of the bruises. I felt like all I had to do was look at something and a wound appeared on my body. I often had so many bruises on my legs that I didn't feel comfortable wearing shorts in the summer. Most people were shocked when they saw the many large marks and would ask how I got them. Because I didn't know, I just laughed it off, explaining I was klutzy and walking into things all the time.

I tried supplements and vitamins as prescribed by doctors, but they didn't stop the marks from appearing. Nothing worked until, with the help of my life energy coaches, I focused on healing the sexual abuse from my uncle and my mom's lack of action related to it. Over the course of several sessions, we focused on transforming the energy behind this trauma. The effect their abuse had on me held me back in so many aspects of my life and I didn't even consciously realize it. I knew the trauma was healed when I felt the need and openness to include the experience in this book. I had not been able to talk about it to anyone, except my sister, but I know now that sharing this experience will help others who have also experienced this kind of abuse.

After each coaching session, I experienced an immediate shift in how I felt inside. I was more peaceful and felt that my inner light was more powerful. My demeanor was much lighter and happier after removing the burden of shame I had carried around for more than four decades. While celebrating my internal victories, I didn't imagine that healing this trauma might also positively affect my outer body.

Shortly after I finished writing about the experience in this book, I looked at my bare legs in the mirror one day and realized I saw not one bruise on them. I can't remember a single day in my life that I had no marks on my legs. I researched the metaphysical cause of bruising and learned that it can be described as a form of self-punishment and feeling guilty about being weak or fragile in certain situations. I immediately drew the connection between the physical manifestation of the bruises and the feelings of helplessness I had toward my uncle and my mom in that situation. The absence of the bruises confirmed that the effects of the abuse had been healed for me. My body was showing up as the perfect partner. Today, I will find the occasional bruise on my body, but I can always identify how I got it.

Were these healings miracles? Of course, they were! They are evidence of our natural healing abilities when we transform our traumas back to love and live from our True Self.

31

RELATIONSHIPS

♥

For much of my adult life, the pain of the relationships I had with my family remained unhealed and continued to manifest in the relationships I attracted. It is odd to see how this plays out but until you transform your negative energy, relationships will continue to show up this way. Connection with others is the most important part of our human existence. Who would we be if we didn't have interactions with others in our lives? Relationships precisely mirror back to us our own level of consciousness and our alignment to our True Self.

We have both good and bad relationships in our lives. While we may at first appreciate only the good ones, we need to learn to value all of them. They are all gifts through which we can learn much about ourselves. A great indicator of how much we love ourselves is through our relationships with others. How others treat you is a very good indication of how you treat yourself. When you are in a state of love for yourself, this vibration can only attract others who will reflect that love back to you.

When you love yourself, you also naturally meet others in the frequency of love.

When you do not fully love yourself, you will attract people who will show you exactly where you are out of alignment with your True Self. For example, in a romantic relationship, you may attract someone who is fully attentive to you, spends time with you, and takes you on trips. They can commit to a monogamous relationship, but they will not make a full commitment for spending their life with you. What they are reflecting to you is your lack of commitment to yourself. This is the time to go within and explore where you are not committed to yourself.

Have you ever reacted strongly to someone in a negative way? Of course, you have. We all come across people who annoy us, who we harshly judge for how they look and act, or for some other negative feeling they bring up in us. We may not even know why we react to them the way we do and we say they "just bug me." We don't want to be around them, and we lament, why can't they be different? We act as victims, putting the blame on them for how they make us feel. Instead, we should thank these people for the gift they are bringing to us. They are showing us where the Ego Mind is projecting that which we don't want to face about ourselves.

They are giving us the opportunity to see where we are out of alignment with our True Self. To quote Eckhart Tolle, "Anything that you resent and strongly react to in another is also in you." Whew, this is a tough one to face when you fully grasp what he means. If you are feeling resistance to this quote, which you probably are, take this opportunity to go within and do the Release Technique on what the statement brings up for you.

While I understood the meaning of the words, it took a long time for me to experientially know what Eckhart Tolle meant. If you are resenting someone because of their sexuality, you should examine your underlying beliefs about sexuality. Perhaps you think that someone is always looking for attention and you judge them harshly for it. Go within and you may discover that as a child you were scolded for trying to stand out in front of others. Judging people negatively solely because they are wealthy is a good indication that you have limiting beliefs about money and you likely don't have much money yourself. You can't judge someone harshly for having something and expect to experience the same thing easily in your own life. That which you judge, judges you back.

Today, I am very aware when I react strongly against another. Having grown up in a very unsafe environment, I quickly became overtaken by my Ego Mind. In its quest to control my world to keep me "safe", it always pointed to people outside of me who were doing me wrong and making me feel bad. I was the ultimate victim on so many layers; unraveling this would take some time.

I now go within to uncover and heal the root cause when I am being triggered by another's action, whether directly or indirectly. This powerful awareness is allowing me to create a more positive inner state, aligned to my True Self, and it is bringing to me more connected and loving relationships.

The most challenging type of relationship for me to heal is romantic relationships. Intimate relationships mirror your alignment with your True Self and this reflection can be painful and heartbreaking. With my parents as relationship role-models, it's no wonder I have been divorced and have had several relationships in my adult life. Before aligning to my True Self, I modeled my mom's narcissistic traits and always had to prove my partner was doing me wrong in some way. I was controlling and manipulative with my partners, fearing both intimacy and abandonment. I was not committed to myself and it showed by my attracting partners who did not commit to me. I am still working on this part of me since the layers run deep, but I am learning to let go of control and I am committed to experiencing true love for myself and for my partner in life.

32

TRUE-SELF EXERCISE

♥

Method: Release Technique for Relationships

Similar to clearing your body using the Release Technique, you can clear the energetic effects of people in your life and heal your relationships with others. You can transform challenging relationships into loving ones in a manner much easier than you imagined.

Think of a person or a group of people with whom you are currently experiencing disharmony but would like to experience more love and connection. This can be a romantic partner, a parent, a friend, a child, a neighbor, coworkers, or a boss. You get the picture; it can be anyone in your life.

How to Practice the Release Technique for Relationships:

1. Begin with the "Connect to Your Heart Space" exercise.
2. Once you have connected to your heart space, picture a brilliant golden light coming down from about two feet above your head. As you breathe in, picture this light coming in through the crown of your head and filling up your entire body.
3. Visualize the person or persons standing before you. Notice how you feel in your body and bring your attention to where you feel discomfort. Keeping your attention on this area, continue to breathe.
4. As thoughts come up, observe them but don't attach to them. Let them go.
5. The feeling of discomfort may shift to other parts of your body. Follow where it goes.
6. Keep breathing until the discomfort has lessened or you can no longer feel it.
7. You may not be able to fully clear an area in a single session. This is completely normal. However, every time you focus on an area, you are moving toward fully releasing the energy that resides there.
8. Once you are finished, return your attention to your heart space and take a few deep, calming breaths.
9. After completing the Release Technique for Relationships, it is very important to send Love to the other person or persons. This may feel strange at first. We may say, "How can I send love to the boss who humiliated me in front of my peers or

the co-worker who took credit for my work? Or the lover who cheated on me or the parent who abandoned me?" We are all connected and when you send love to them, you are also sending love to yourself. You are celebrating that you are healing negative emotions and situations between the two of you.

While remaining focused on your heart space, visualize the person or persons in front of you and say to them out loud or in your mind:

> "*Person's name*, I recognize you as your True Self and I am thankful for all the gifts our relationship has brought to me. I forgive you, I celebrate you, and I send love to you!"

What comes up when you are doing the Release Technique is what needs to heal for this relationship. You may get visions of other people. This shows a connection to the unhealed relationship. Just breathe through it, do not attach to it or expand on it, and keep releasing whatever comes up.

Do not get upset if you are not able to let go. Relationships are powerful and bring up a lot of buried feelings. Many times, your Ego Mind will present well-crafted stories around the connections because it does not want to change them. It wants to feel picked on, imposed upon, and just in its thought. It wants to judge ourselves and others. Over time and with practice you will be able to recognize when the Ego Mind is at play, and it will be easier to release without attaching to its story.

33

COURAGE & RESILIENCY

♥

The Merriam-Webster dictionary defines courage as the "mental or moral strength to venture, persevere, and withstand danger, fear or difficulty." Courage is when we are willing to take on something that is hard or challenging. We boldly attempt an effort because we feel the rewards are worth the risk.

Per the American Psychological Association, resilience is defined as the process of adapting well in the face of adversity, trauma, tragedy, threats, or significant sources of stress—such as family and relationship problems, serious health problems, or workplace and financial stressors. It's our ability to bounce back quickly when we experience hardships in our lives.

Courage and resiliency go hand in hand. Courage is an act we do proactively to overcome that which we want to conquer in our lives. Resilience is how we react to events that happen to us. I believe both are necessary traits to have as you expand into your True Self.

Brené Brown's definition of courage resonates deeply with me: "Courage is a heart word. The root of the word courage is cor – the Latin word for heart. In one of its earliest forms, the word courage meant to speak one's mind by telling one's heart. Over time this definition was changed, and today, we typically associate courage with heroic and brave deeds."

For many of us, the mere thought of letting others see us for who we truly are is downright terrifying. Baring our hearts, really exposing our self to another, is one of the most courageous acts we can do. Writing this book is a daring undertaking for me, because I come out not only about my beliefs but also about my childhood experiences. Both are parts of myself I wanted to keep hidden from others when I was living in fear. Having grown up in conditions where I had to hide to stay safe, exposing my authentic self puts me in the ultimate state of vulnerability.

Throughout my life, I embodied courage and resiliency to overcome deep poverty, homelessness, and heartbreak. Aligning to my True Self, I made the choice to move toward positive experiences rather than remain in adverse situations. Advancing forward in life comes from a place of self-love. It requires a deep commitment to work through the fear that may accompany it.

My biggest act of courage was embarking on the journey to discover who I really am. On my healing path, I have accelerated my transformation. With courage, I look at everything within me not aligned to my True Self. I willingly walk into the depths of suffering in order to rise to the heights of love, peace, and joy.

My journey to know my True Self is an expedition; I am a pioneer setting out to discover the unknown. While others have come before me, I am blazing a new, unique trail, just like you and others who will follow us. There are almost 7.8 billion people on this planet and there will be 7.8 billion individual paths to awakening to the True Self. This is your call to set out on your journey.

I don't always like what I learn about myself. Our Ego Minds always want to make us right and convince us that everyone else is wrong. The Ego Mind gains power through our victimhood. When I started seeing patterns of what I was doing to others, when my less-than-loving behavior came to the light, I will admit I was shocked that I wasn't always the good person my Ego Mind told me I was. I thought a lot of bad things had been done to me by other people, but I could now clearly see my alignment to those actions.

As I expand my consciousness and align to my True Self, I dive headfirst into facing the negative patterns within myself. I push through the pain that comes with the awareness, willingly exposing more and more causes of my suffering. Sometimes healing comes fast; other times it feels like a Band-Aid being slowly ripped off. We have deep layers of hurt and trauma to unravel, created through our own life experiences and from ancestral beliefs programmed within our DNA.

Each step you take in aligning to your True Self, especially the first one, is a powerful and courageous move. I discovered that just by setting the intention to commit to the change, your transformation will move more easily and elegantly than if you were resisting it. The hardest step is to change how you think about yourself. You are not a victim of circumstance. You are not locked forever into who you are today. You are a powerful creator who can rapidly change yourself and your experience in this world.

When we have the courage to see ourselves in a different light, anything is possible. Change can be scary. Who we have been and what we've experienced may be painful, but it's known and there is comfort in familiarity. Embarking on a new path can be daunting but I challenge you to consider it from the angle of courage. See life as an expedition and picture yourself as an adventurer setting off to find a new world. Because that is exactly what you are going to create, a whole new reality for yourself.

34

FORGIVENESS

♥

Forgiveness is a courageous act that is often misunderstood. Many people believe it means you accept when someone has done you wrong, and you condone what they have done to you. In fact, forgiveness is not at all about the other person, but it is something you do for yourself. Per the Greater Good Science Center at the University of California, Berkeley, forgiveness is generally defined by psychologists as "a conscious, deliberate decision to release feelings of resentment or vengeance toward a person or group who has harmed you, regardless of whether they actually deserve your forgiveness."

From a life energy perspective, relieving yourself from the low vibrations of resentment and vengeance is necessary to align to your True Self. As long as you feel you cannot forgive, you will remain stuck in this low energy. It's only when you forgive that you can return to the high vibration of love.

Forgiving does not mean you accept, gloss over, or deny what was done to you. It doesn't mean forgetting, either. You are not obligated to maintain a relationship with those who have hurt you, but forgiveness does allow you to place boundaries between yourself and the wrongdoer, whether you completely shut them out of your life or continue to have a relationship with them. You forgive out of love for yourself.

You may say, wait, there is NO WAY I can forgive what someone did to me that was so hurtful and betraying. I am here to tell you, YES, YOU CAN, and you *must* if you want to be free from the low vibration energy associated with the painful act.

I deliberately left this section until the end of the book. I felt it important to share my story with you so you can understand the depth of suffering I experienced from my parents. As I healed myself, I came to realize my father's physical abuse of my mom absolutely contributed to her state of mental health. I have compassion for the terrors she must have faced at his hands and how scary it must have been for her when he killed himself, leaving her alone with no means to take care of us children. I understand my father became an abuser and alcoholic due to growing up with an abusive parent. My parents' Ego Minds fed off each other, creating a vicious cycle of pain they could only escape by taking their own lives. They didn't know any better and they didn't know their True Selves.

I will never have the opportunity to talk to my parents as an adult. I would love to share the wisdom I have gained and experience healing together with them. But this is not our destiny in this lifetime. All I can do is face the trauma and adversity I experienced so I can heal myself to stop the effect of destructive behaviors from moving forward.

I have fully forgiven everyone who played a part in the abuses and adverse experiences they helped co-create in my experience. Through healing the traumas and subsequent limiting beliefs that were stuck deep within me, I began to see the role I played in every experience through the eyes of my True Self. Being aligned to who I really am allows me to look at what occurred from a higher perspective. I am able to see the part everyone else played in my own expansion of consciousness and how they prepared me to step into my roles of teacher and coach. I feel only love for them, and I see them as their True Selves.

Forgiving myself has been the hardest act of all; of everyone in my life, I am the hardest on myself. When I was a child, I felt it was my fault my parents behaved as they did toward me. I thought I wasn't doing something right and maybe it would be better if I weren't there. I have not respected myself for some of my past behaviors and how I treated others. For most of my life, I felt unworthy of expecting anyone, even myself, to give to me out of love rather than from an ulterior motive. I felt I did not deserve to be celebrated by others just for being who I am.

As I heal the past trauma, I learn we are all doing our best, given our level of consciousness, and before I can expect anyone to love or celebrate me, I must first love and celebrate myself. I cannot attract and sustain loving relationships if I am feeling unworthy toward myself.

I want you to also consider forgiveness from this point of view: We attract into our experience that which is aligned to the vibration of our life energy. When we are aligned to love, that which shows up is positive and loving. When we are out of alignment, that which shows up is negative and hurtful. There is just no getting around it.

You may protest that you didn't ask for negative situations that have shown up in your life. "I didn't ask for my husband to cheat", "I didn't want the car accident", or "I didn't make myself lose my job." Of course, you didn't consciously want those things; no one wants to have bad things happen to them. Your life energy was aligned to the low energy of these adverse situations, causing you to manifest them in your life. When you are not consciously aware of the beliefs held in your subconscious mind or the level of your energetic vibration, you don't realize you are a receptor for these negative experiences.

When someone does us wrong, if we shift our perspective from being a victim of the act to seeing ourselves as the attractor of the experience, we can free ourselves from suffering. We can instead see the experience as a red flag showing us exactly where we ourselves are out of alignment to our True Self. We can then proactively heal that which is non-loving to loving. Instead of hate, we can now show gratitude to the wrongdoer for showing us our disconnection from love. Gratitude is on the other side of the spectrum from fear and hate. Embodying gratitude allows us to stay connected to our True Self.

35

LETTING GO

♥

The tools and techniques I have provided will work when you are able to let go of what does not serve you. Letting go is challenging. Our Ego Mind loves drama. It clings to our stories and to people who may not be right for us. It keeps us safe while it creates our limited identity. It is difficult to let go of the familiar – the personal baggage, the job title, the relationship, or the idea of yourself as a victim. Most of us find comfort in the known, but the payoff is huge if we can learn to trust in our transformation and let go. Letting go means we are putting our faith in something bigger than ourselves when we head into the unknown.

When you work through the techniques I share in this book, you will encounter internal resistance along the way. The Ego Mind will create situations that distract you from your desires. The avoidance can show up in many ways: procrastination, inability to focus, overeating, working long hours, or making yourself unconscious via alcohol or drugs. Believe me, as someone who would regularly drink a couple glasses of wine at night, I am an expert on the things we do to resist growth.

I desired moving into my career of life energy coaching for years, but it meant coming out about my beliefs to many people who don't share my beliefs. Some will laugh at me, ridicule me, or scorn me. Yet I know there are many others who will applaud me and love me for living my truth. Others will resonate with my story and learn from the wisdom I have gained. My fear of not being supported through this change kept me repeating unhealthy behaviors. Only when I fully made a commitment to myself could I say "no!" to the acts that kept me away from starting my coaching business.

Letting go means trusting. Trusting God, trusting your True Self, and trusting others. Expecting that what you need will show up when you need it. Letting go means really paying attention to what comes up for you when you do the exercises in this book. It means not creating a story about what manifests but looking for the clues that will enable the positive shift you desire.

People will fall out of your life. You will first mourn the losses, but you will find much more joy in learning to release them. While you may love those who go, they are no longer aligned with who you are and therefore, by the natural laws of the universe, they must leave your life. You can try to hold on to them out of fear but doing so will only delay the inevitable separation while creating unneeded pain and suffering.

Letting go means not worrying about how what you want is going to come into your life. It means allowing all the good you desire to come to you. When you are connected to your True Self, to the light within, you have no reason to fear things will not be aligned with what you want. By following the True-Self exercises in this book, you will have all the tools you need to move into a higher vibrational version of you.

When you let go, the results will be beyond your wildest dreams. Look at my life. Look at where I started and where I am today. If I had never set out on the journey to find my True Self; if I hadn't listened to my light when I was twenty-one years old, pushing me toward a better future; if I hadn't learned how to let go of what my Ego Mind was telling me, I would not have experienced the life I have so far. I would not be positioned to receive what I am creating for the future.

I am so grateful for the abundance I have been able to experience in my life. I am the mother of two beautiful girls. I've worked for amazing companies and participated in the gifts of service they bring to the world. The people I've met have been diverse and interesting. I've known love and friendships. I live in a beautiful coastal community in California. I have a new Mercedes-Benz sedan that is fun to drive and always reliable. Contrary to my childhood expectations, I've traveled by plane to almost every state in the United States and visited countries like Japan, Kenya, and French Polynesia.

Letting go means taking your hands off the handbrakes to allow what you want to come into your life. It is through this surrender that you will experience the greatest freedom to create an extraordinary life.

36

TRUE-SELF EXERCISE

Putting It All Together

The exercises in this book will allow you to experience the power of your True Self. Love is at the root of every exercise, since we connect to God through our heart. You can experience great results just by using one or two techniques on a regular basis, but you become a divine powerhouse when you combine them all to create your desired result.

I recommend becoming familiar with all the techniques and trying out various combinations to see what works best for you. Below is an example of how you can combine the methods to turn Loneliness into Connection:

- Begin with the "Connect to Your Heart Space" exercise.
- Practice gratitude for the loneliness and the lessons you learned from it.

- Use the Release Technique to clear the feeling of loneliness from your body.
- Create an affirmation for replacing the loneliness with positive relationships. For example, "I AM always experiencing loving relationships."
- Use the Release Technique to clear resistance to the affirmation in your body.
- Visualize what "loving relationships" look like for you. Generate how good it feels to have this connection with other people.
- Practice gratitude for the relationships.
- As you go about your day, set the intention for loving experiences as you move from one situation to the next.

As you become more familiar with the True-Self exercises, you may gravitate toward using some techniques more than others. Have fun trying out different combinations of the techniques. In the next chapter, I share with you how I used multiple True-Self exercises to help me get through my lifelong fear of public speaking.

37

OVERCOMING FEAR OF PUBLIC SPEAKING WITH TRUE-SELF EXERCISES

♥

Public speaking is something I really love to do; the moments I have done it well have filled me with joy. For most of my life, I was a master at hiding and avoiding the limelight, so I never really honed this skill. Like many people, I experienced anxiety at just the thought of speaking in front of other people, although the depth of my fear was likely more pronounced due to my unhealed traumas. When I graduated college, I took a job in marketing specifically because it required that I regularly present technical demos as part of a sales team. In that role, I traveled around the country to meet with different customers on a daily basis. I soon was able to speak to people everywhere I went but I always had to manage an underlying sense of anxiety and uneasiness.

My next career move landed me in a software engineering role, where I no longer needed to speak in front of others. As time passed and I became out of practice,

OVERCOMING FEAR OF PUBLIC SPEAKING WITH TRUE-SELF EXERCISES

I developed even more anxiety, sometimes downright panic, at the thought of doing a presentation. Engineers spend more time with technology than people, focused in deep concentration to solve technical challenges. It's not surprising that the longer I was an engineer, the more introverted I became.

Over the next few jobs, I was able to stay mostly in the background until there came a point in my career where I needed to be front-and-center in a big way. I was chosen to manage a high-profile project that required me to regularly present complex technology topics to large groups of stakeholders and peers.

Anxiety is created by projecting limiting beliefs and fears into the future. I realized I needed to counter that energy and create an atmosphere where I could bring to myself that which I wanted to create. I wanted to present myself to my stakeholders and peers as someone who communicates well and knows what they are doing; someone you could trust, who is capable, and is the right person to lead this large endeavor. I couldn't let my deep fright of public speaking get the best of me.

Following my inner guidance, I created the affirmation: "I AM a powerful, engaging, articulate, and confident public speaker." When I repeated the affirmation, I watched what came up for me in my thoughts and feelings. Was I resisting or feeling negatively in any way? Since the need to hide goes back to early childhood, there were many layers of resistance to get through. I had to repeat this process several times for each speaking experience.

Prior to each talk, I visualized giving a dynamic presentation, with people coming up after to congratulate me on the project or tell me how much they enjoyed my talk. My boss would praise me for the presentation, exclaiming how well it went with our important stakeholders. I also conjured up how it would feel within my body to be successful.

While driving to work in the morning, I repeated the affirmation to prepare my energy for the day. Five minutes before a presentation, I retreated to a quiet place to practice my affirmation and check in with how my body felt. Sometimes a stall in the ladies' room was the only private spot I could find. I would set my intention, repeat the affirmation, and release all the tension and anxiety that arose. I felt like a ball of nerves while heading into the conference room and sat with knots in my stomach, until it was my turn to present. I continued repeating the affirmation in my head while I waited.

When it was my turn to speak, something magical happened. As I started talking, all the anxiety immediately fell away, and I presented my topic with ease. Every talk went smoothly and always ended on a positive note.

This approach worked in even the most stressful circumstances. One particular time, I was called to give an overview of my team's part in a very large and difficult cross-functional initiative. There were more than 75 attendees, including the very intimidating senior executive who was leading the overall effort. The other presenters were visibly nervous and had a strong desire to please the senior executive. He inevitably took them to task about one thing or another, not letting them off the hook for the slightest infraction.

I silently practiced my affirmations while watching the others. When it was my turn to present, my talk went smoothly and effortlessly and was met with the senior executive's praise. Afterward, one of his top staff members approached to tell me how much he enjoyed my presentation, declaring he was especially impressed with how confident and calm I appeared.

If you suffer from the fear of public speaking, I encourage you to try this method the next time you need to give a talk. You may need to practice this approach multiple times since different situations bring up different levels of anxiety. For example, a meeting with a few peers may be very easy for you, presenting an important topic to your boss could elicit strong anxiety, and the idea of presenting to a large crowd has you cowering in fear. Keep working with the process and I guarantee that over time, probably faster than you anticipate, you will be able to easily and calmly speak in front of others with less stress and anxiety than you face today.

38

YOUR LIFE WILL BECOME EXTRAORDINARY

———— ♥ ————

As you heal, you will view the circumstances in your life from a different perspective. What you once deemed bad will now have a deeper meaning, and you will see the gift in it. You will feel love and understanding for all others, where before there was hate and judgment.

I truly believe if you are reading this book, you are ready to awaken to your True Self. Some people may not want to know themselves this way yet. They are afraid to end their suffering. It gives them identity, something to latch onto in this fleeting existence. They can't let go. It scares them to contemplate possessing a power they have been raised to believe is only reserved for an unseen god or savior. But this power is in us all; those of us who experienced trauma and those who felt ease in life. We are all truly equal to each other; there are no winners or losers, and competition only exists in the Ego Mind.

Many will be scared when they hear that they create their own reality. "I didn't create this disease, this poverty, this bad relationship!" they will exclaim. "Do you think I wanted the illness in my body; that I asked for it?" They will challenge you, coming from their Ego Mind instead of their heart space. Instead of marveling at the power within them, they will cling to their old way of thinking. They may be afraid they did something wrong and that their God might punish them.

As you live from the magnificence of your True Self, you will be amazed at the events, people, things, and feelings that appear in your life. For me, the greatest gift I manifested is being in a state of calm and inner peace most of the time. I no longer live with debilitating anxiety and deep worry. I can write comfortably in front of others. It's uncommon for my body to react with shaking or sweating during situations I once labeled distressing. My breath flows freely, my body feels loose, and I stopped grinding my teeth at night. This transformation has made my life extraordinary.

I am no longer afraid of death because I have come to know myself as the divine, infinite being that I am. I choose to live my life accepting there are risks, rather than being stopped dead in my tracks by the fear of mortality. I am here in this life to experience it all, good and bad. I am here to grow in consciousness. I don't listen to others' limiting beliefs about life expectancy or the degradation of health and life quality as we age. I know when we align with the powerful force of love, only that which is loving can show up in our experience. From this perspective, I live in freedom, not fear.

Expanding into your True Self may be deemed selfish by some people, but it is not. You have to take care of yourself first. In fact, you cannot do this for anyone else and no one can do it for you. You have to do the work to align with your True Self. Others can help you through your transformation by holding space and channeling high vibrational life energy, but you must be the one to experience the effects of the healing.

You are on this planet to expand and grow. You will never be done. You will keep evolving. However, when you release and transform a past trauma or a limiting belief, you will never need to do it again. Healed by divine energy is healed for good.

Some people will see your evolution as a call for them to awaken and expand. You will become a leader in this transformation of humankind. Others who are not ready for this change may hold firm to their limited beliefs about their reality, no matter what you tell them or show them. They will label deliberate manifestations a coincidence or just plain luck. They are not yet ready to grasp that this is a reality they could experience as well. It's okay. They are okay. Trust that they are okay, and release them from judgment. See them for their True Selves and trust that they, too, will be supported in their life.

This is a journey we are on together, yet we are each on a unique path in different stages. It's not always easy. You have to do the work. You will experience blessings when you release all that is not aligned with your True Self. Becoming aware of why things are happening will increase your power. You are no longer a victim of circumstance. You are now able to see yourself as a powerful creator and can consciously shift to create something different.

My desire to write this book came from my True Self and who I came here to be, a beacon of light to show you how magnificent you are. My wish is that my story will give you the hope that you, too, can overcome adverse experiences and powerfully create a new life for yourself.

YOUR LIFE WILL BECOME EXTRAORDINARY

When you connect with your True Self, I am confident you will experience an extraordinary life, one that is greater than your wildest dreams, created by you and for you.

ACKNOWLEDGEMENTS

♥

First, I want to thank my parents for being powerful co-creators of my life experience, allowing me to grow in consciousness and to learn the true meaning of love. I picture the two of you, on the other side, high fiving each other in celebration of this book. Thank you for being a part of my journey. I love you both and I see you for your True Selves.

I am deeply grateful for my beautiful daughters, who give me so much love and so many opportunities for growth each day. I love the two of you more than I could have ever imagined loving anyone. I am so blessed to be your mother.

To my sister, the only person who really understands what I endured in my childhood: Thank you for the times you loved me, protected me, and took care of me as only a big sister could.

To my nephew and niece: I am so grateful to you; your unwavering love has been a bright spot during the deepest challenges of my life. I've had the gift of sharing that love with you as I watched you grow from beautiful babies into the amazing people and parents you are today.

To all my teachers and coaches on my path to knowing my True Self: I would not be where I am today without your amazing support and guidance as we transformed my pain back to love, healing my past. Thank you for sharing your truly amazing gifts with me.

And lastly, I am grateful for everyone who has ever been or still is a part of my life. Whether our experiences together were judged as good or bad, I am so grateful for having you in my life. I have learned so much about life and about myself from each of you.

RESOURCES

Life Energy Coaching

If you would like to explore how you can further expand your transformation to your True Self, please visit Amy at Calm Ocean Coaching www.calmoceancoaching.com. Here you can find information on individual and group coaching programs, energy transformation products, and Amy's blog.

True-Self Exercise Recordings

Audio recordings for all True-Self Exercises included in this book can be found at www.calmoceancoaching.com/true-self-exercises.

ABOUT THE AUTHOR

Amy Blakeslee is a certified life energy coach and founder of Calm Ocean Coaching, Inc., where she works with executives to realize their unlimited potential by connecting to their True Self. Leveraging the methods described in this book combined with leading-edge life energy techniques, Amy guides enlightened leaders through the transformation needed to create phenomenal results both personally and professionally. Helping others return to an inner state of peace and calm is at the heart of Amy's work.

Amy enjoyed a successful 25+ year career in the Information Technology field. She has a Bachelor of Science degree in Information Technology from DeVry University, starting her career as an engineer and progressing to executive leadership roles in Data and Analytics technology. Her experience spans multiple industries at major corporations, including The Walt Disney Company, Universal Music Group, Hyatt Hotels, and Raytheon Company.

Amy lives in Southern California, with her two daughters and their dog, Talulah.

Made in the USA
Las Vegas, NV
16 September 2021